FIRST 50
RELAXING SONGS

YOU SHOULD PLAY ON THE PIANO

ISBN 978-1-5400-8152-0

HAL•LEONARD®

Visit Hal Leonard Online at
www.halleonard.com

Contact Us:
Hal Leonard
7777 West Bluemound Road
Milwaukee, WI 53213
Email: info@halleonard.com

In Europe contact:
Hal Leonard Europe Limited
42 Wigmore Street
Marylebone, London, W1U 2RN
Email: info@halleonardeurope.com

In Australia contact:
Hal Leonard Australia Pty. Ltd.
4 Lentara Court
Cheltenham, Victoria, 3192 Australia
Email: info@halleonard.com.au

CONTENTS

BELLA'S LULLABY

from the Summit Entertainment film TWILIGHT

By CARTER BURWELL

Moderately

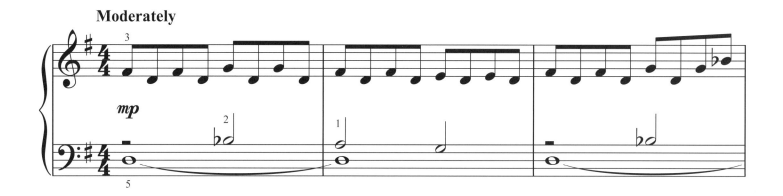

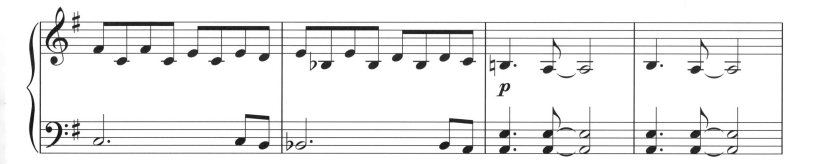

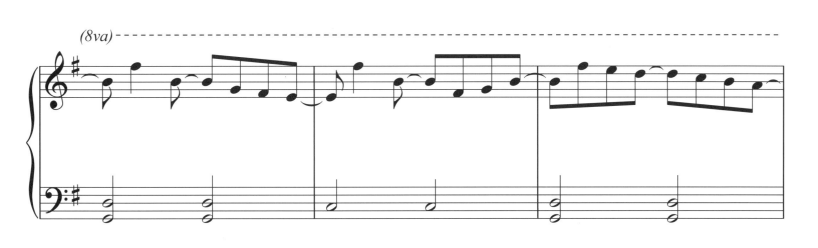

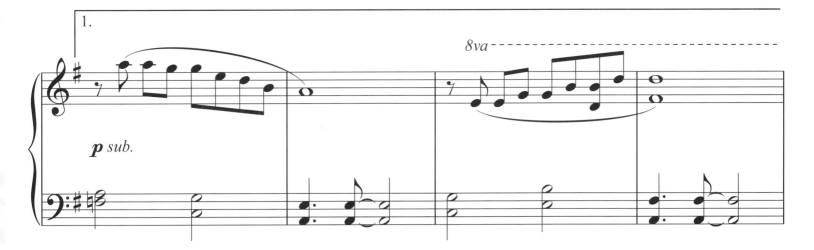

AND SO IT GOES

Words and Music by
BILLY JOEL

Slow Ballad, with much rubato

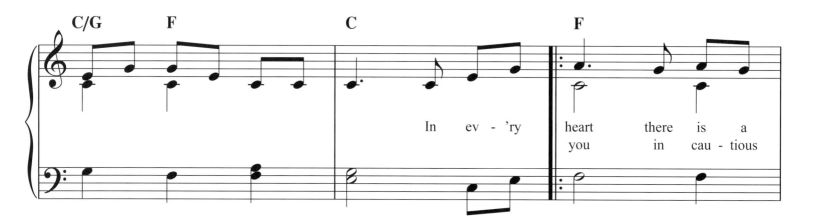

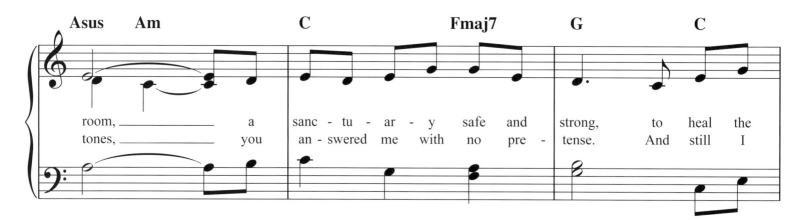

In ev - 'ry heart there is a
you in cau - tious

room, _____ a sanc - tu - ar - y safe and strong, to heal the
tones, _____ you an - swered me with no pre - tense. And still I

wounds from lov - ers past, _____ un - til a new one comes a -
feel I said too much. _____ My si - lence is my self de -

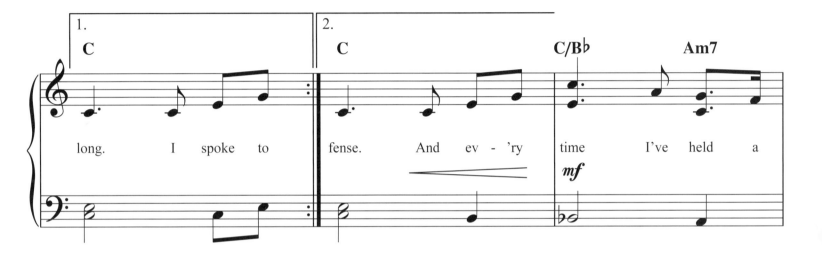

long. I spoke to
fense. And ev - 'ry time I've held a

rose it seems I on - ly felt the thorns. _____ And so it

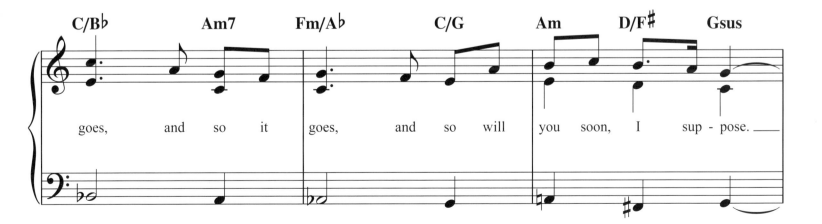

goes, and so it goes, and so will you soon, I sup - pose. _____

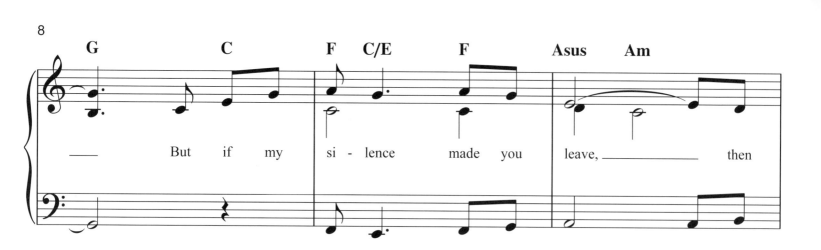

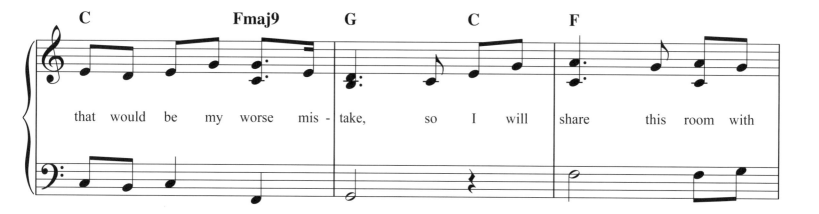

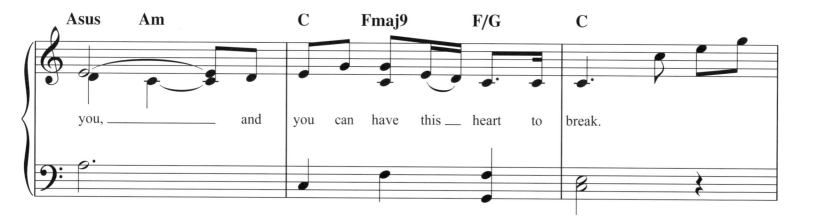

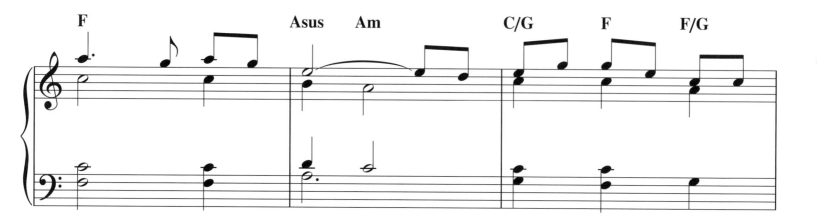

And this is why my eyes are closed; it's just as

well, for all I've seen. And so it goes, and so it

goes, and you're the on - ly one who knows. So I would

choose to be with you. That's if the choice were mine to

make. But you can make de - ci - sions too, _____ and

you can have this __ heart to break.

And so it goes, and so it

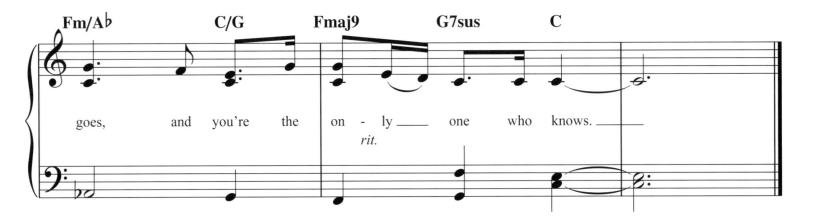

goes, and you're the on - ly ___ one who knows. ___

rit.

BLOWIN' IN THE WIND

Words and Music by
BOB DYLAN

Moderately

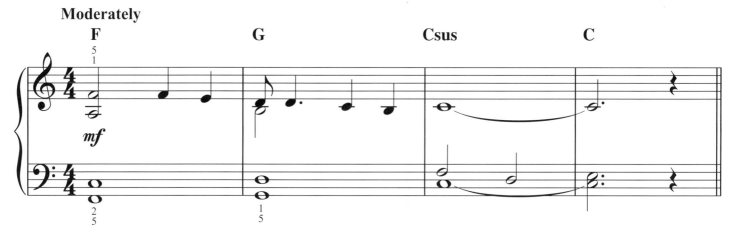

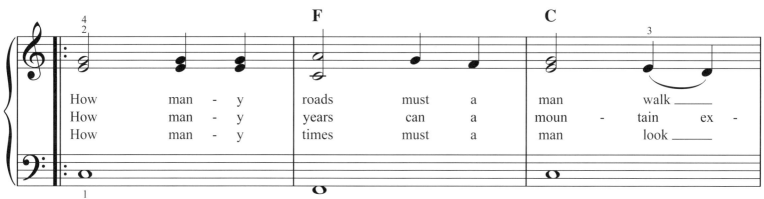

How man - y roads must a man walk _____
How man - y years can a moun - tain ex -
How man - y times must a man look _____

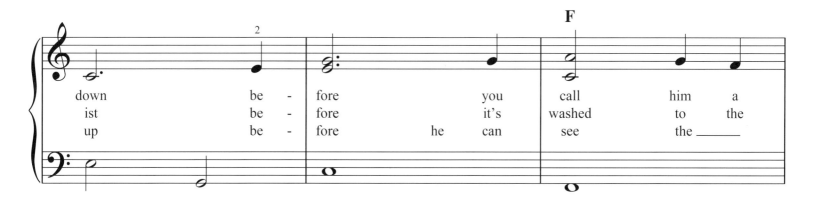

down be - fore you call him a
ist be - fore it's washed to the
up be - fore he can see the _____

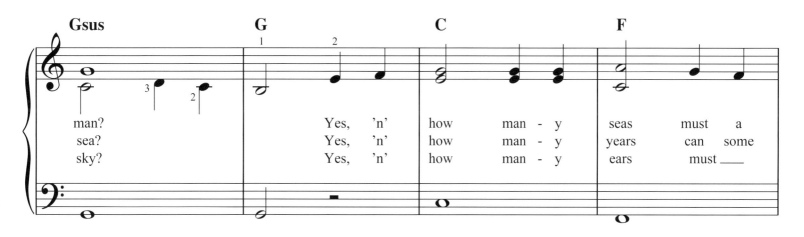

man? Yes, 'n' how man - y seas must a
sea? Yes, 'n' how man - y years can some
sky? Yes, 'n' how man - y ears must _____

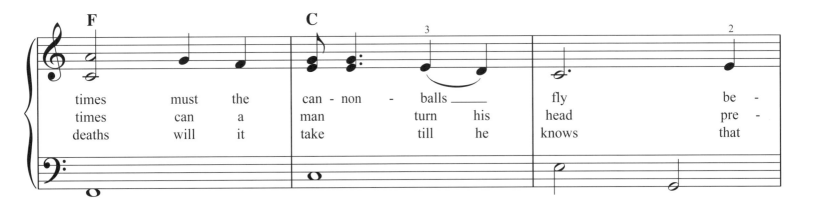

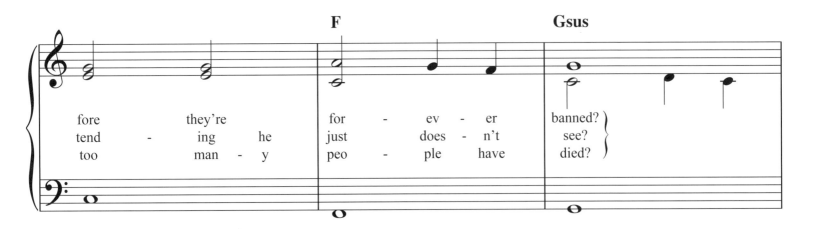

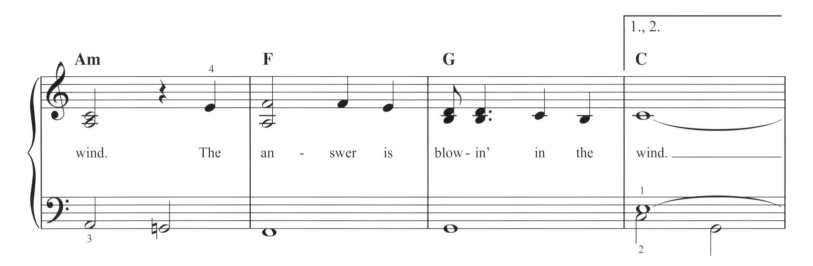

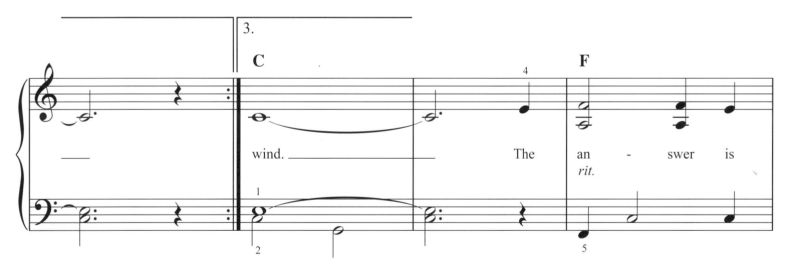

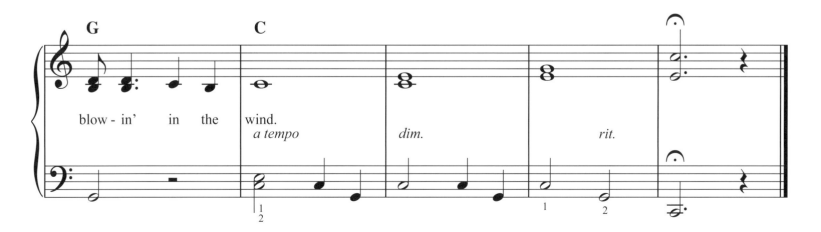

ANNIE'S SONG

Words and Music by
JOHN DENVER

With motion

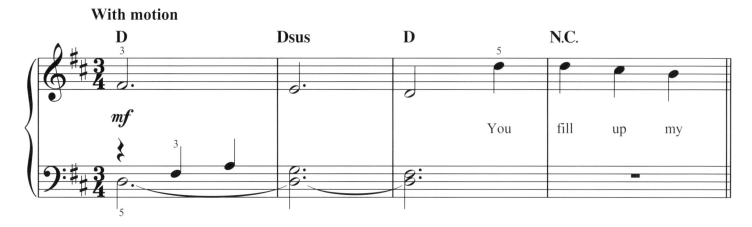

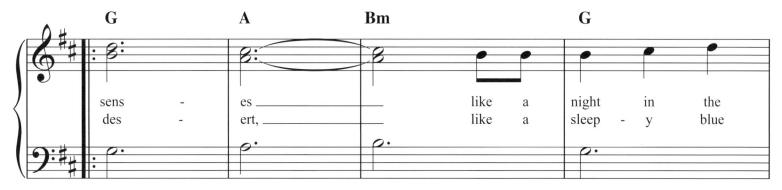

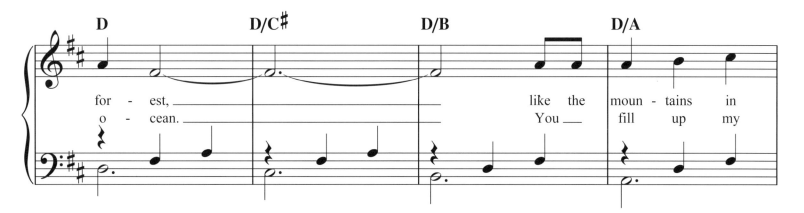

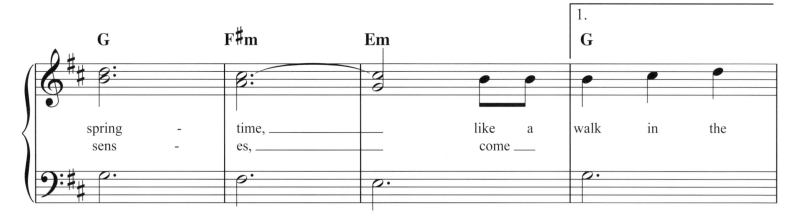

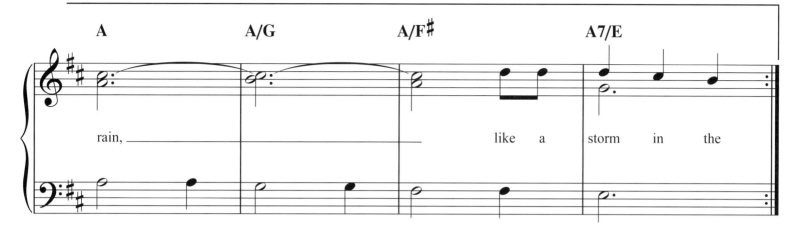

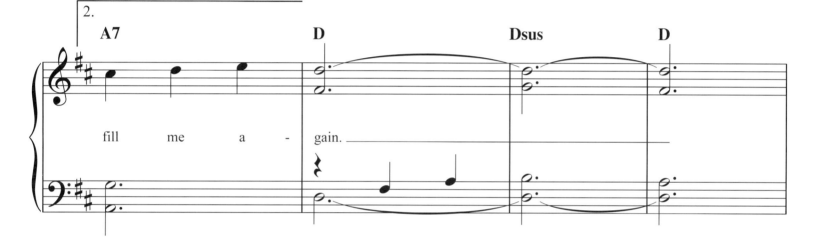

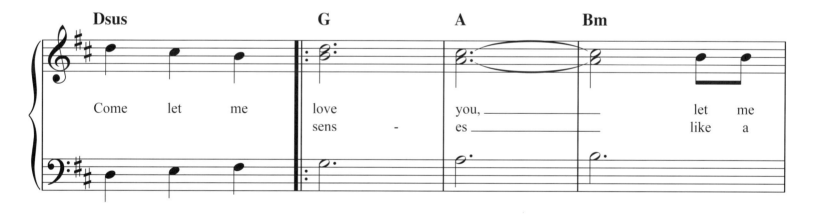

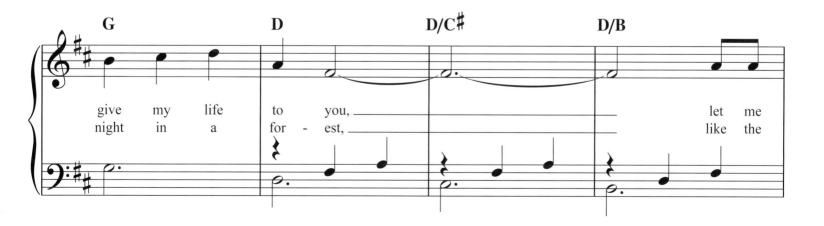

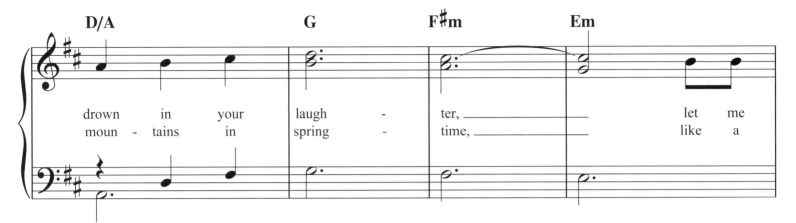

drown in your | laugh - ter, _____ | let me
moun - tains your in | spring - time, _____ | like a

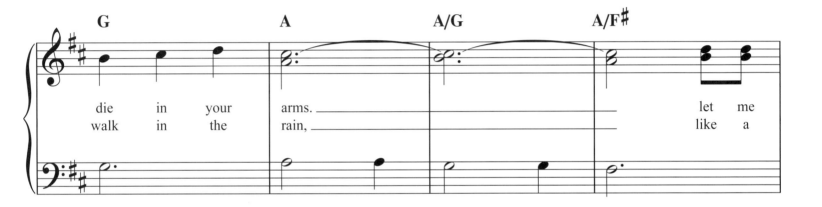

die in your | arms. _____ | let me
walk in the | rain, _____ | like a

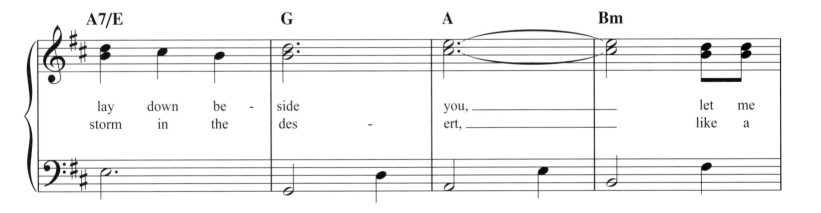

lay down be - side | you, _____ | let me
storm in the | des - ert, _____ | like a

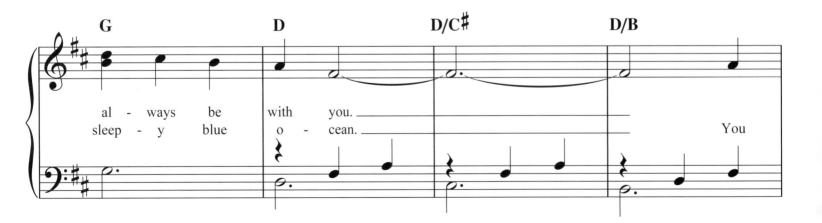

al - ways be | with you. _____ |
sleep - y blue | o - cean. _____ | You

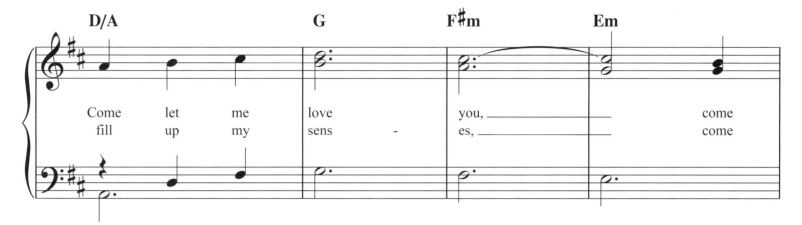

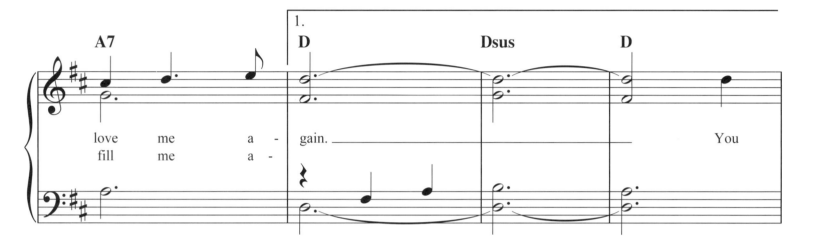

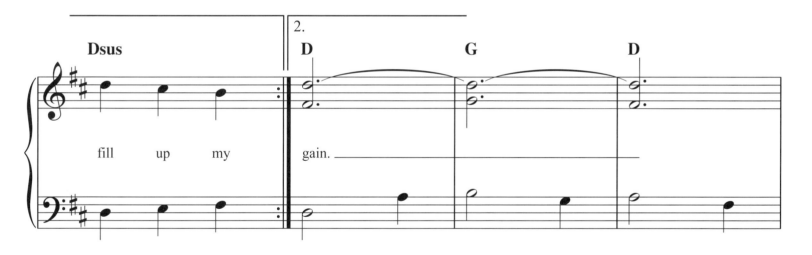

BLUE MOON

Music by RICHARD RODGERS
Lyrics by LORENZ HART

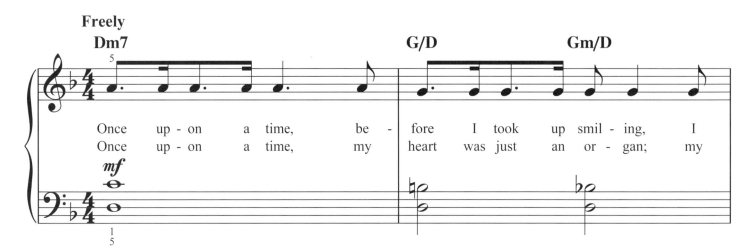

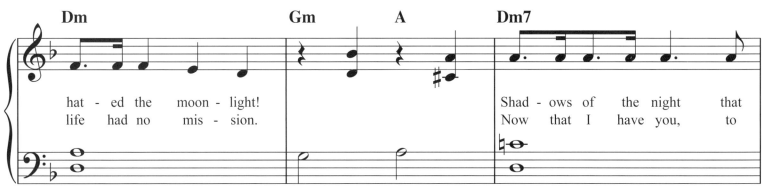

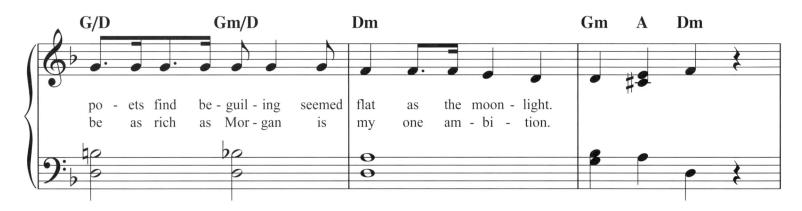

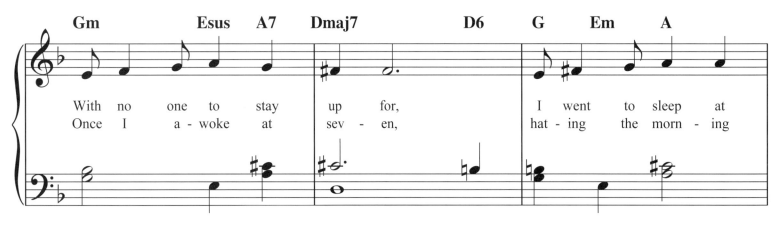

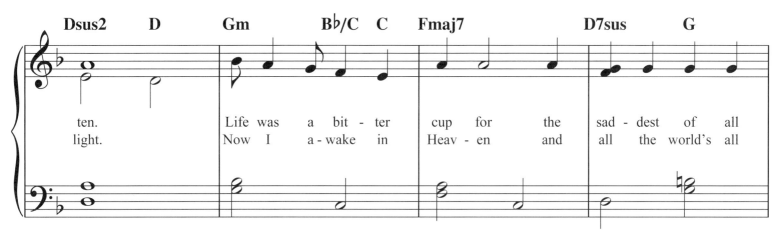

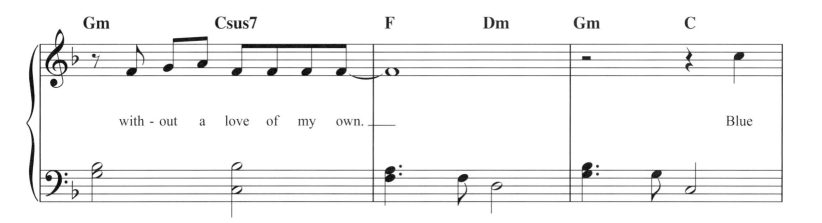

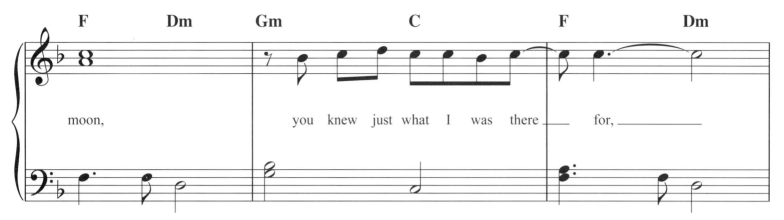

moon, you knew just what I was there ___ for, _____

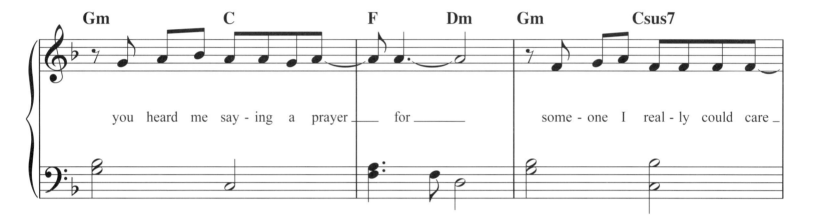

you heard me say - ing a prayer ___ for _____ some - one I real - ly could care _

___ for. And then there sud - den - ly ap - peared be -

fore me _____ the on - ly one my arms will ev - er hold. _____ I heard some -

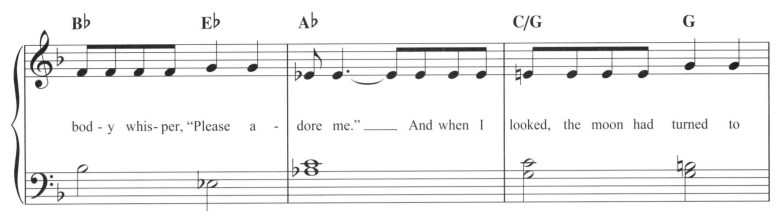

bod - y whis-per, "Please a - dore me." ____ And when I looked, the moon had turned to

gold! Blue moon! Now I'm no long - er a - lone, __

____ with-out a dream in my heart, ___ with-out a love of my own. __

____ *rit.* ____ *rit.*

BOTH SIDES NOW

Words and Music by
JONI MITCHELL

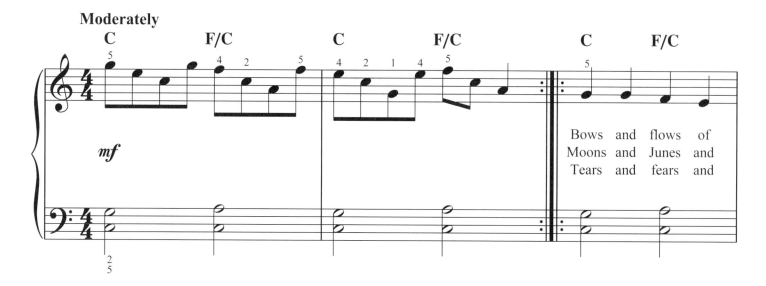

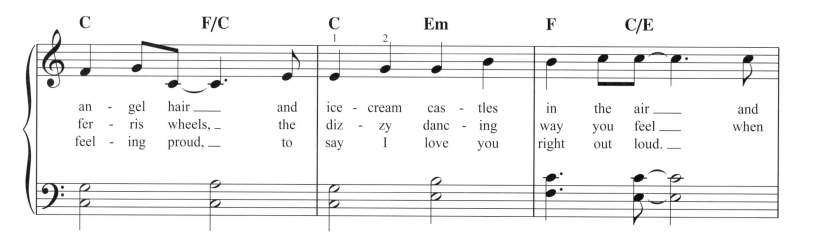

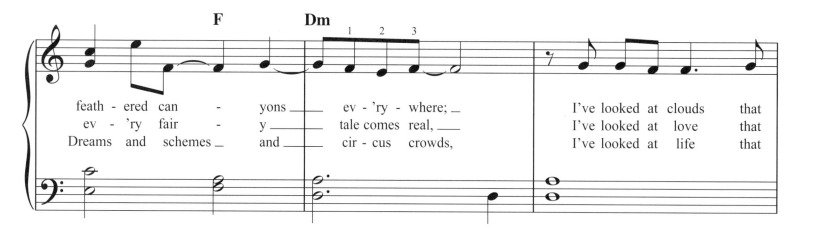

way.   But now they on - ly   block the sun, ____ they
way.   But now it's just an - oth - er show. ____ You
way.   But now old friends are act - ing strange, _ they

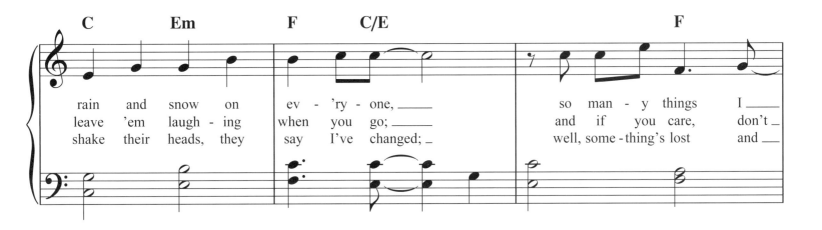

rain and snow on   ev - 'ry - one, ____ so man - y things I ____
leave 'em laugh - ing when you go; ____ and if you care, don't _
shake their heads, they say I've changed; _ well, some - thing's lost and ____

____ would have done,   but clouds ___ got in my way.   I've
____ let them know,   don't give ___ your - self a - way.   I've
____ some - thing's gained in liv - ing ev - 'ry day.   I've

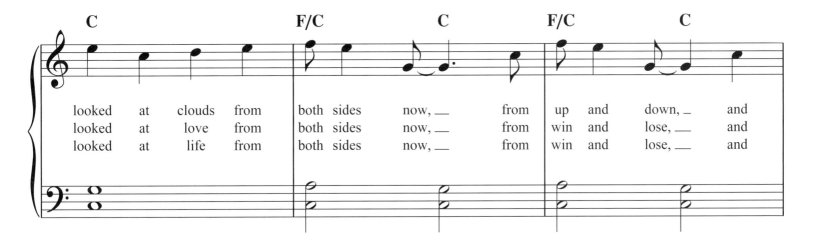

looked at clouds from both sides now, ___ from up and down, _ and
looked at love from both sides now, ___ from win and lose, ___ and
looked at life from both sides now, ___ from win and lose, ___ and

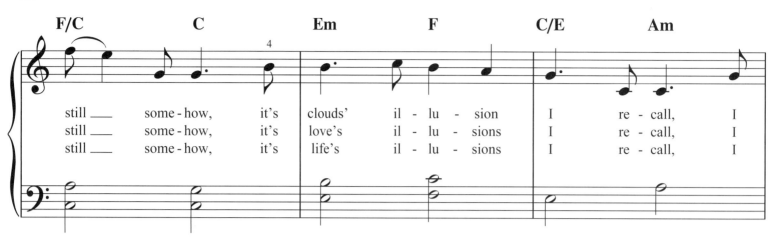

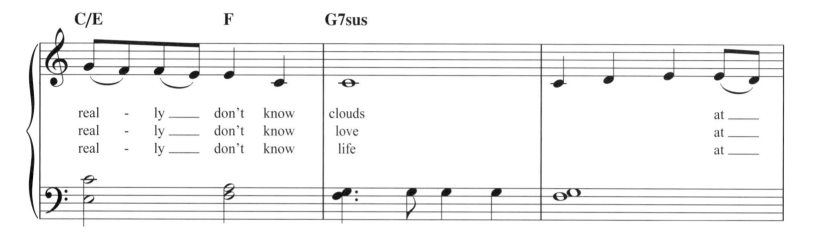

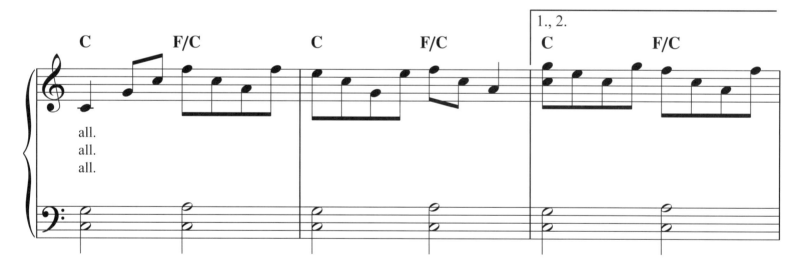

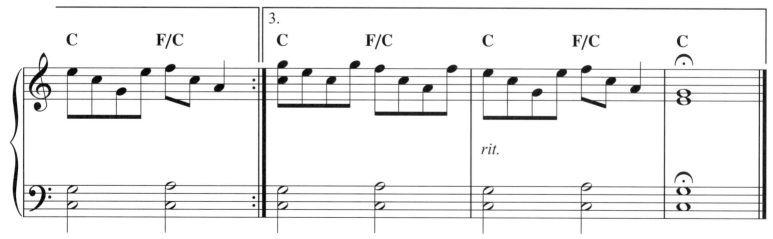

BRIAN'S SONG
Theme from the Screen Gems Television Production BRIAN'S SONG

Music by MICHEL LEGRAND

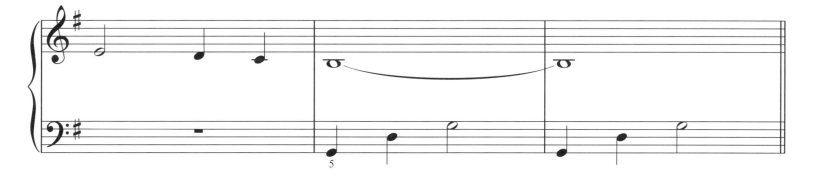

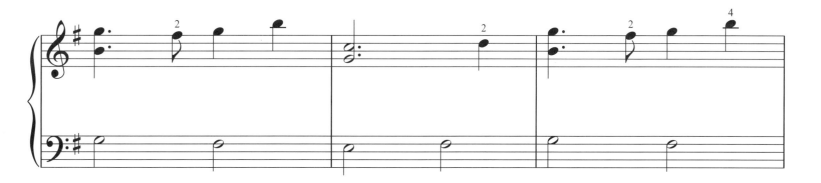

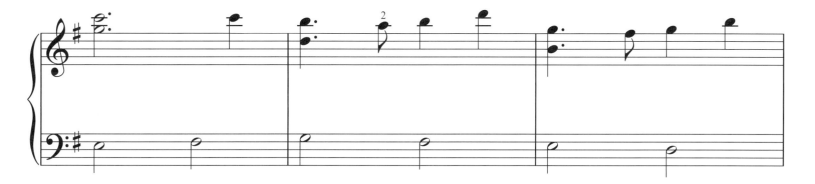

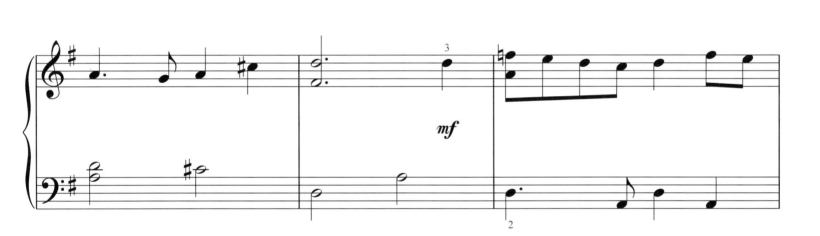

CAVATINA

from the Universal Pictures and EMI Films Presentation THE DEER HUNTER

By STANLEY MYERS

Slowly, with feeling

To Coda ⊕

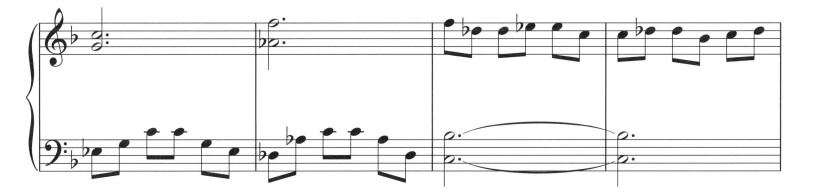

poco rit.   a tempo

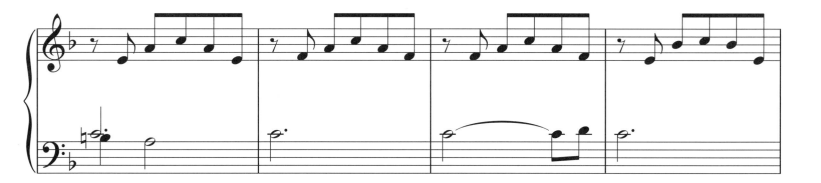

D.C. al Coda

CODA

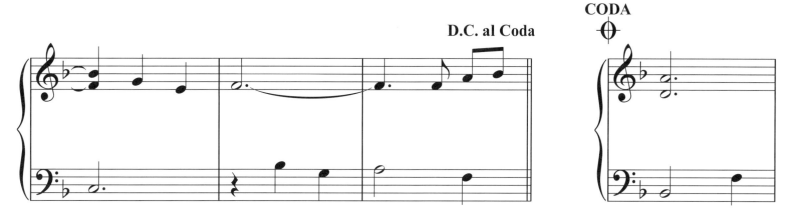

CHARIOTS OF FIRE

from the Feature Film CHARIOTS OF FIRE

By VANGELIS

Moderately slow

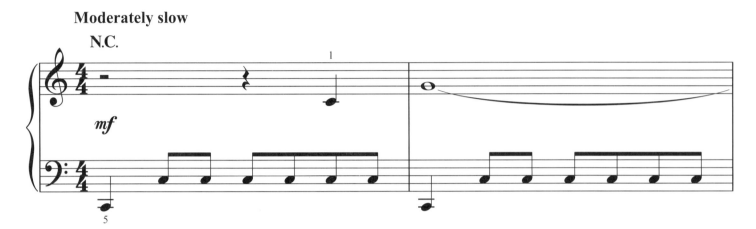

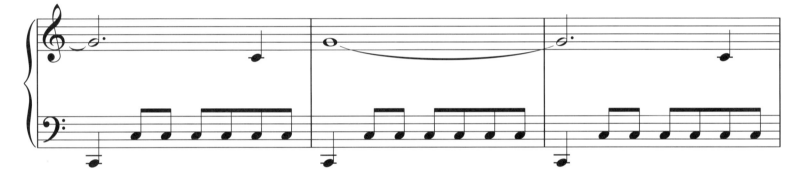

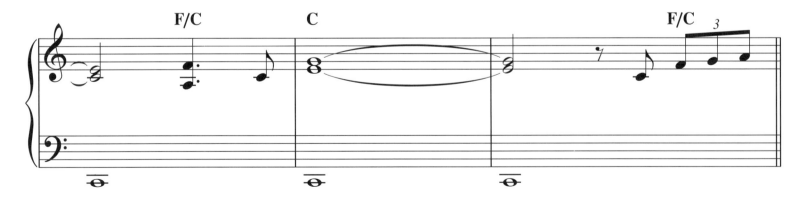

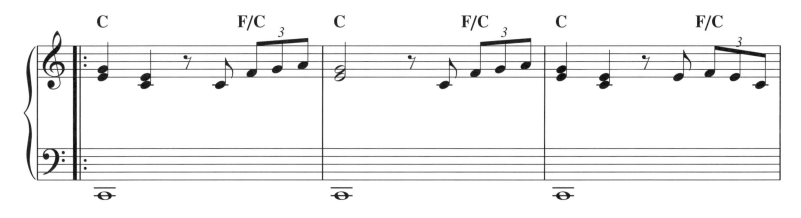

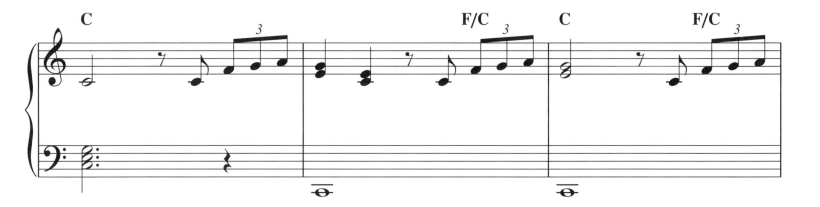

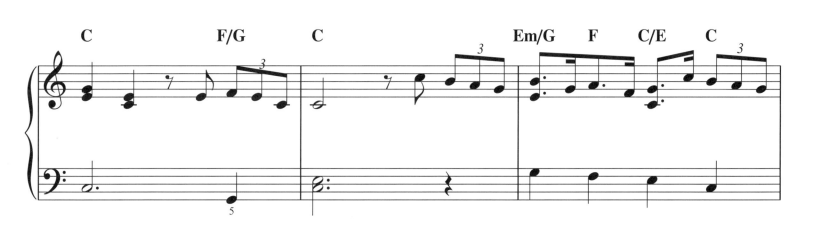

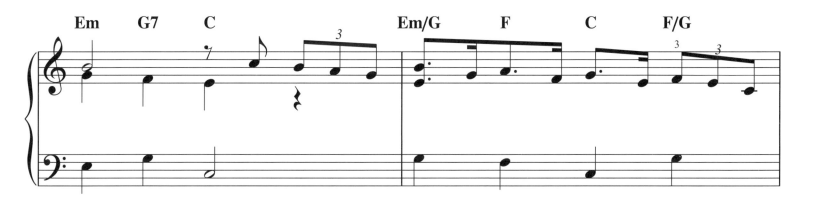

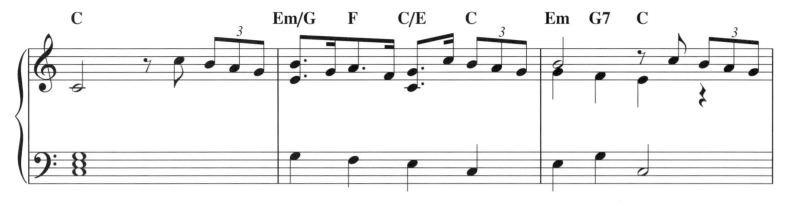

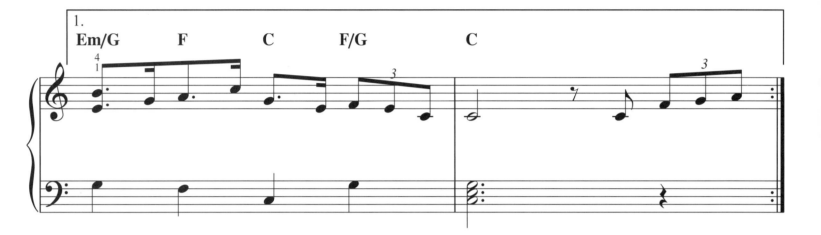

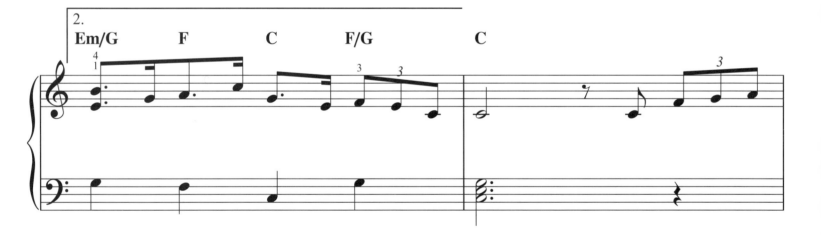

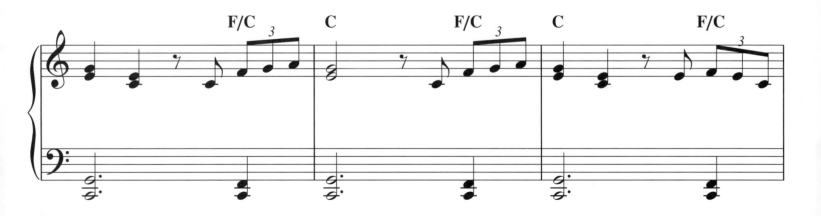

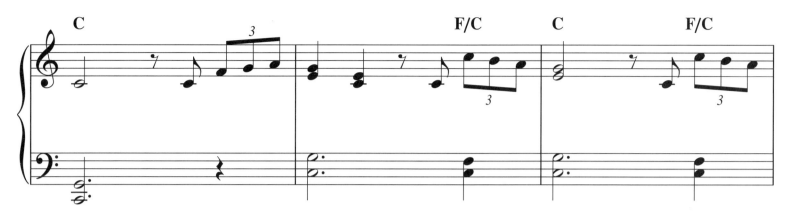

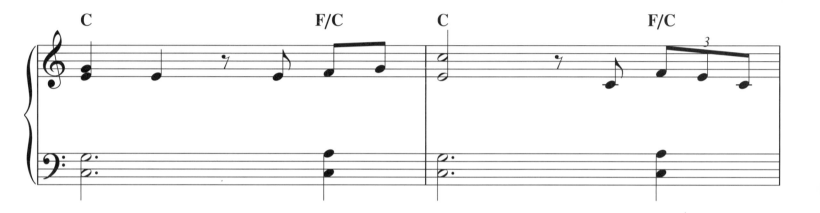

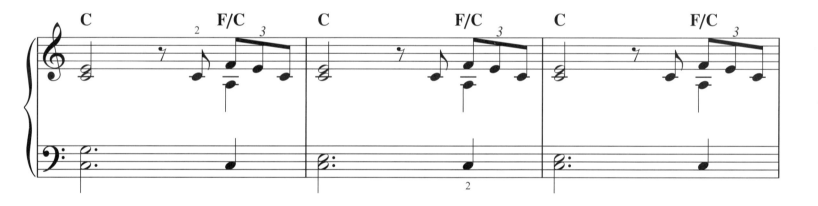

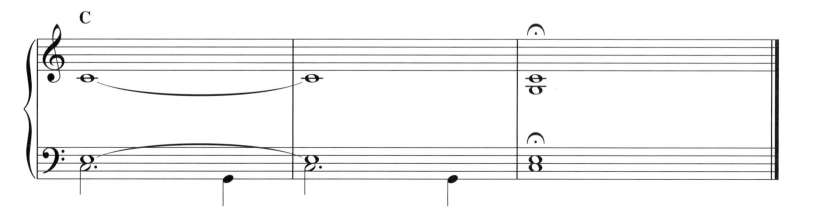

CINEMA PARADISO

from CINEMA PARADISO

By ENNIO MORRICONE
and ANDREA MORRICONE

Moderately slow, with feeling

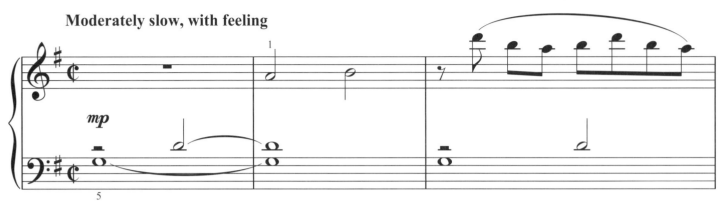

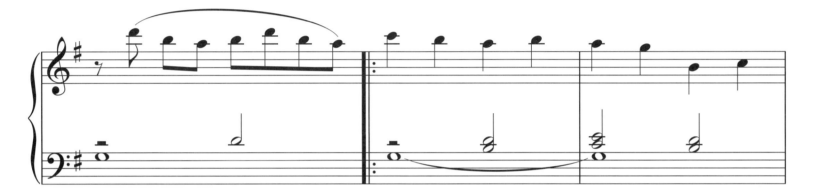

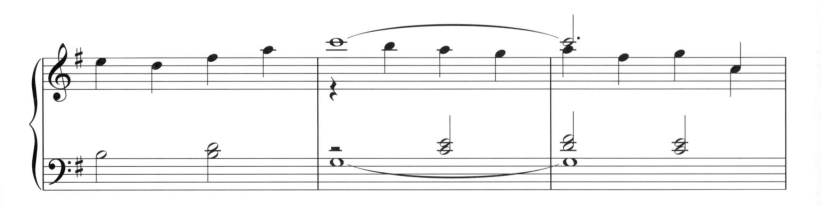

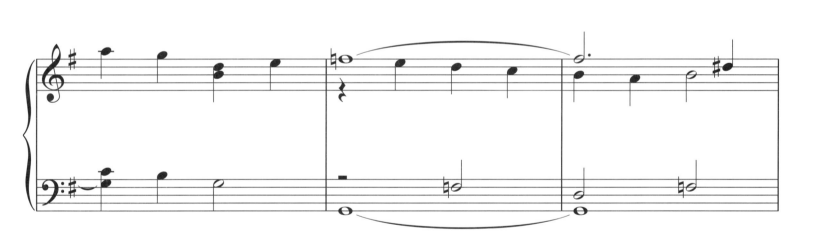

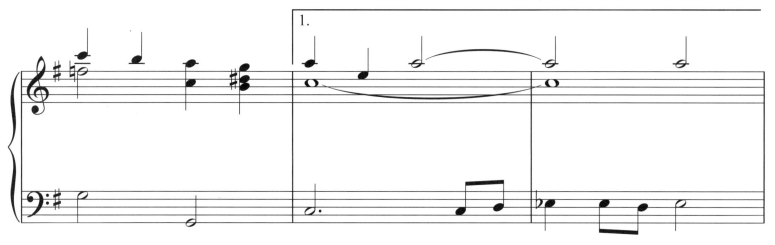

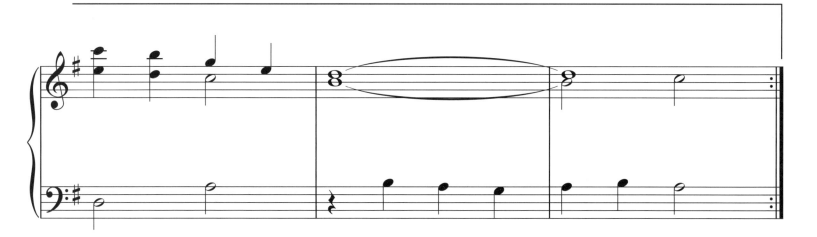

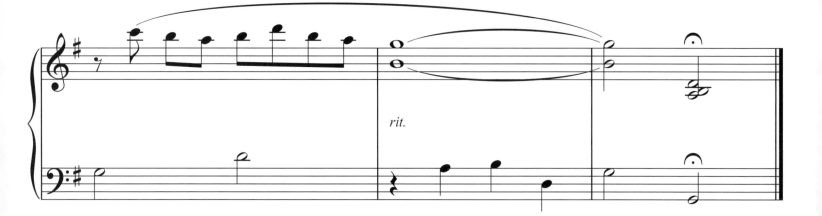

(They Long to Be)
CLOSE TO YOU

Lyrics by HAL DAVID
Music by BURT BACHARACH

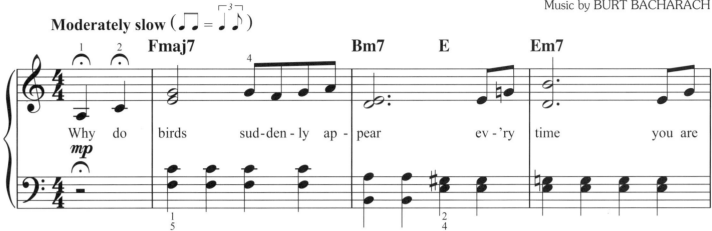

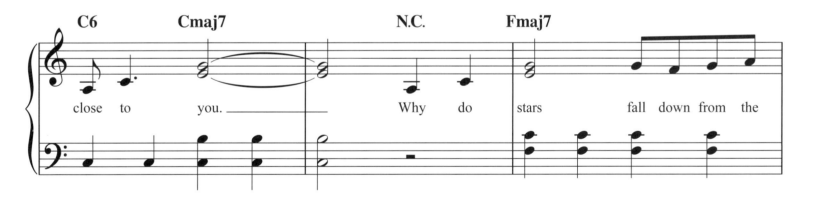

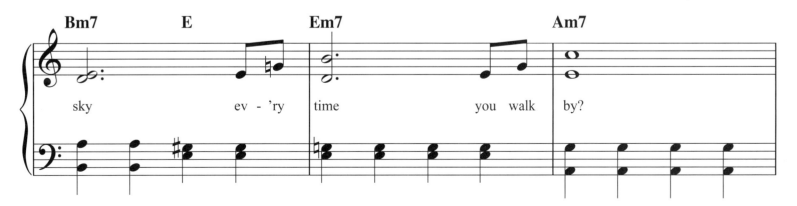

Just like me, they long to be close to you. ____

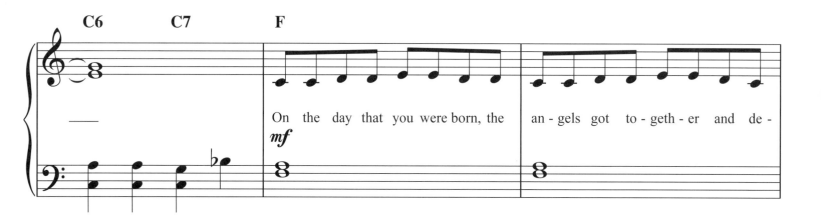

____ On the day that you were born, the an-gels got to-geth-er and de-

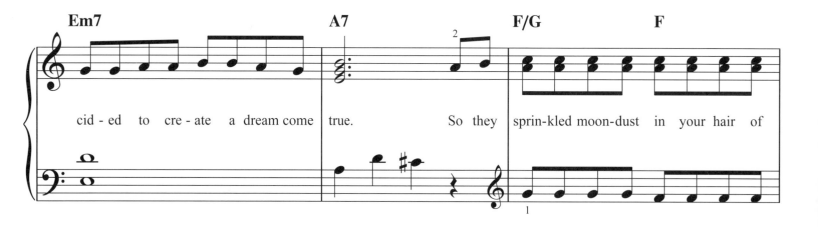

cid-ed to cre-ate a dream come true. So they sprin-kled moon-dust in your hair of

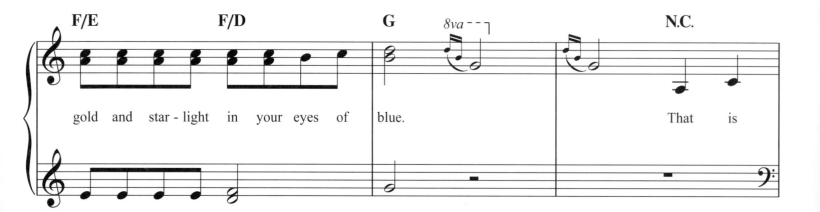

gold and star-light in your eyes of blue. That is

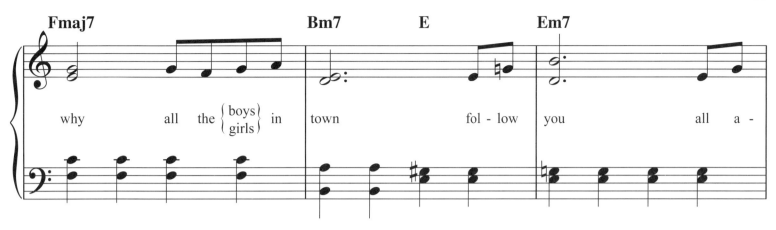

why all the { boys girls } in town fol-low you all a-

round. Just like me, they long to be

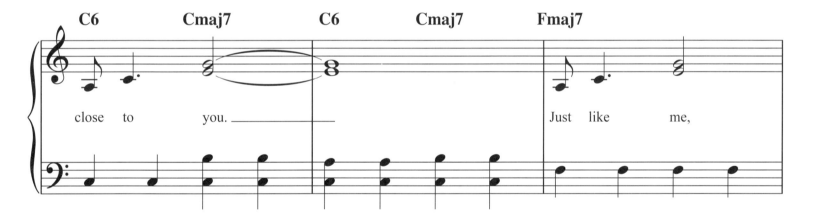

close to you. _____ Just like me,

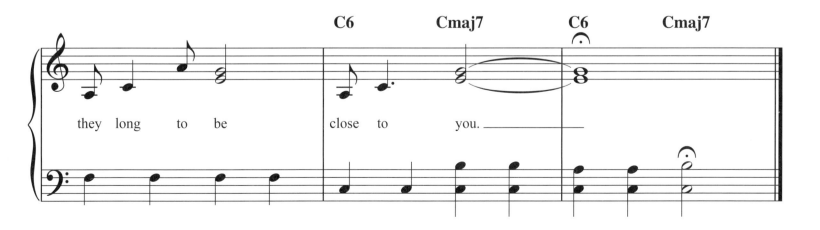

they long to be close to you. _____

COME AWAY WITH ME

Words and Music by
NORAH JONES

Moderately slow

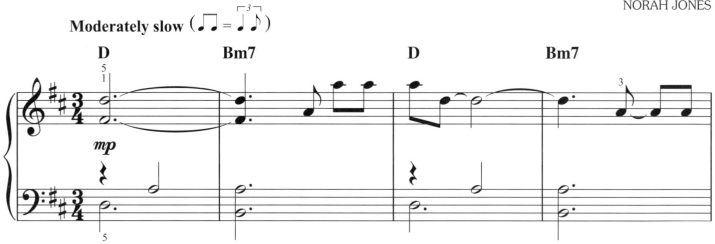

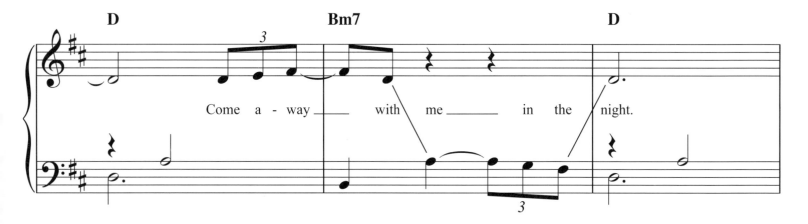

Come a - way ____ with me ____ in the night.

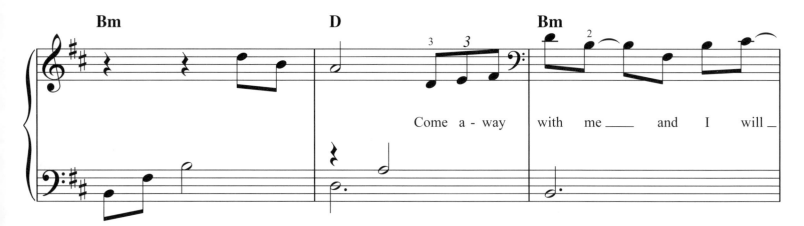

Come a - way with me ____ and I will ____

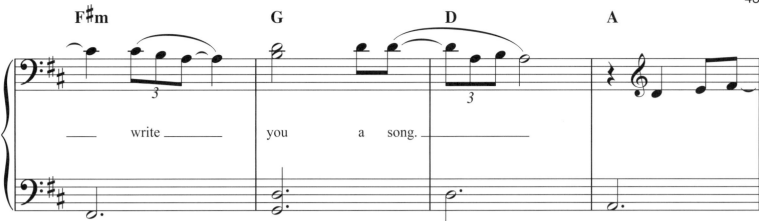

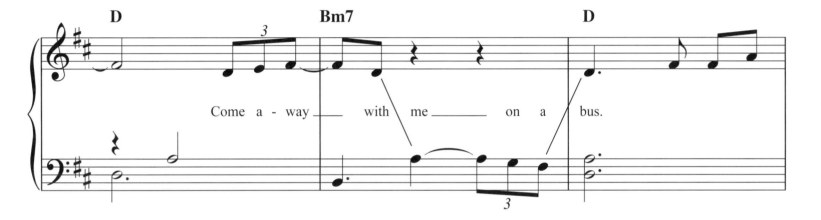

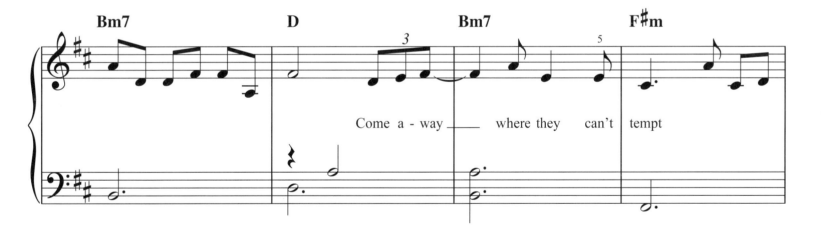

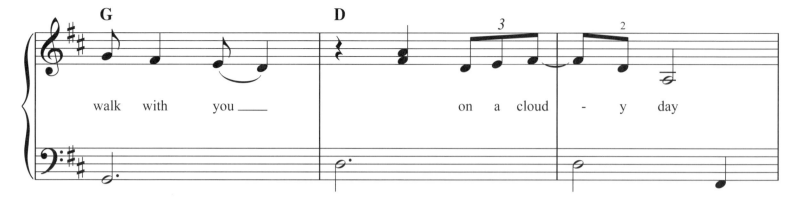

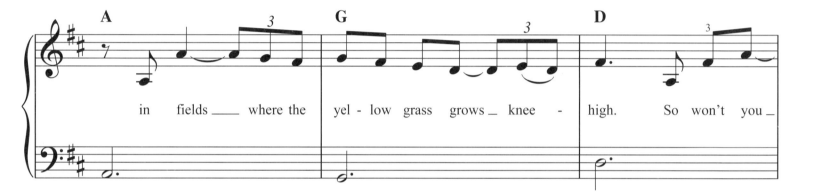

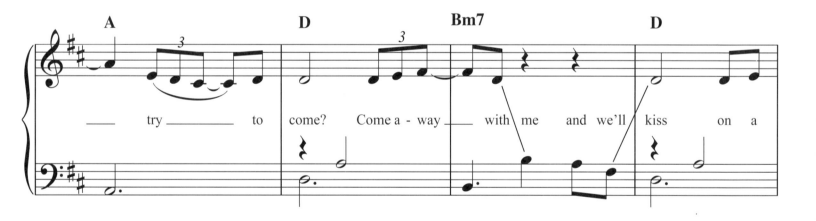

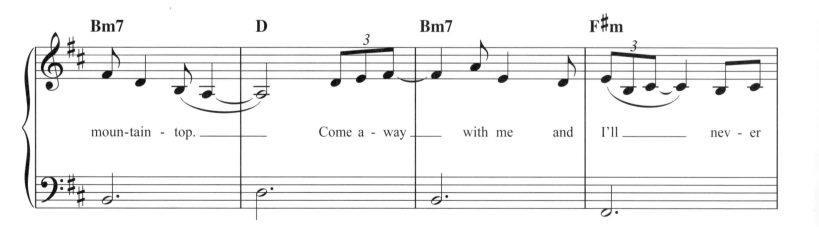

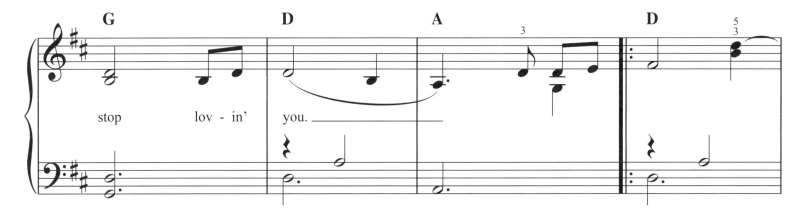

stop   lov - in'   you. _____

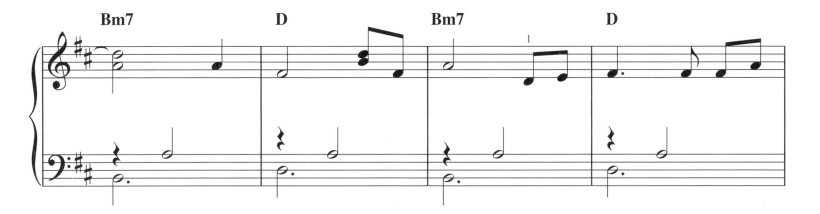

And I _____ wan-na

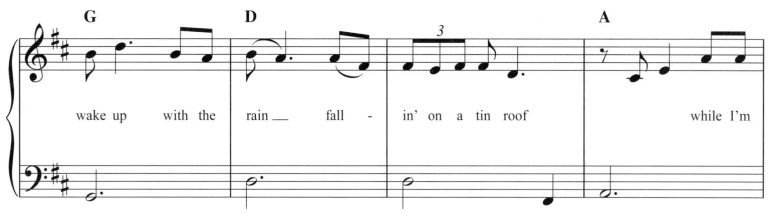

wake up   with the   rain____   fall -   in' on a tin roof   while I'm

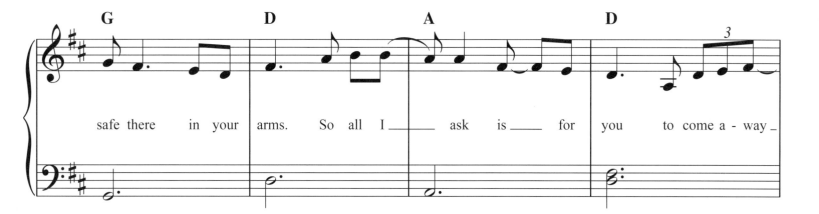

safe there   in your   arms.   So all I ____   ask is ____   for   you   to come a - way ____

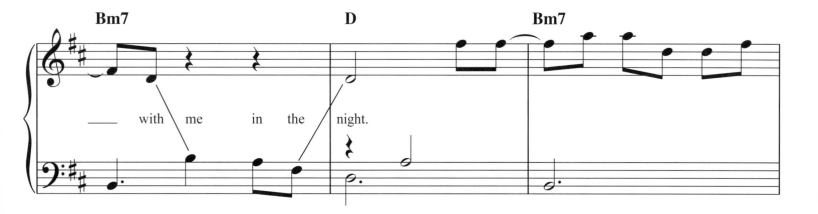

____ with me   in the   night.

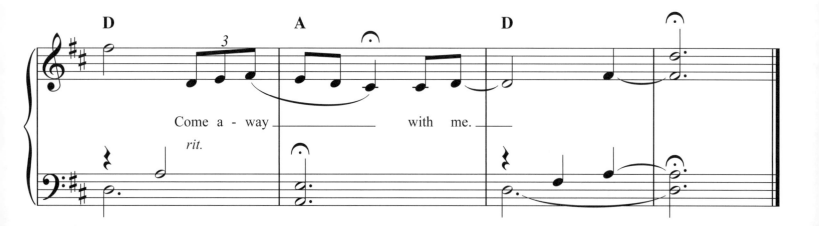

Come a - way _____   with me. ____

rit.

DAYS OF WINE AND ROSES

from DAYS OF WINE AND ROSES

Lyrics by JOHNNY MERCER
Music by HENRY MANCINI

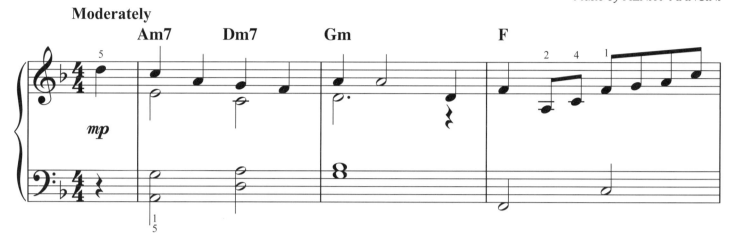

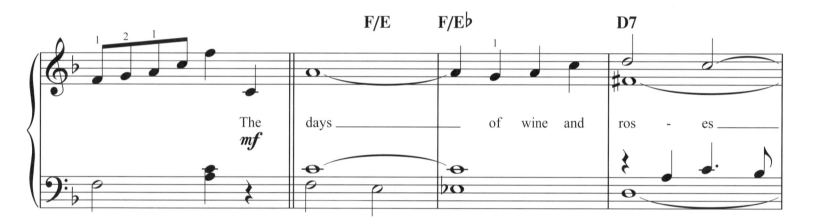

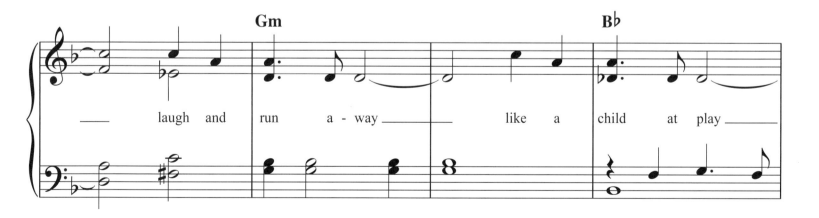

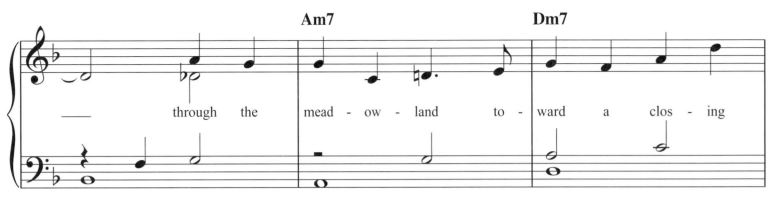

through the mead - ow - land to - ward a clos - ing

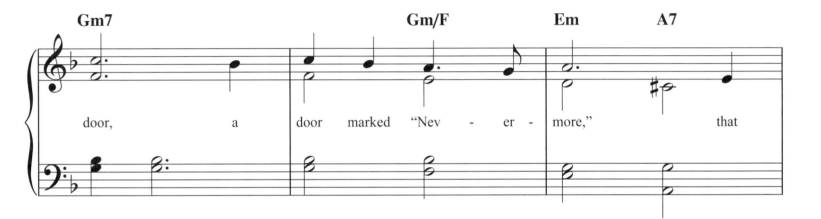

door, a door marked "Nev - er - more," that

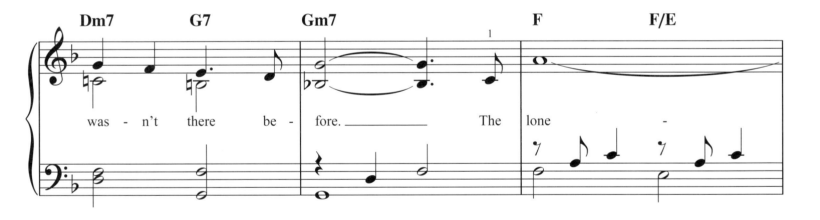

was - n't there be - fore. The lone

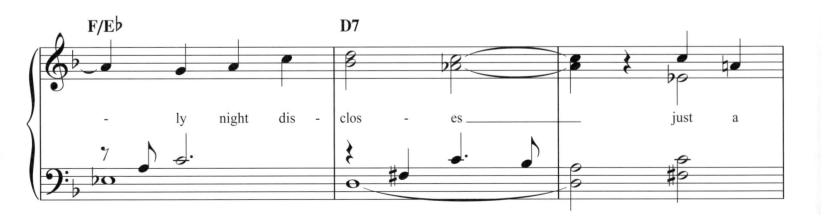

- ly night dis - clos - es just a

pass - ing breeze   filled   with   mem - o - ries _____

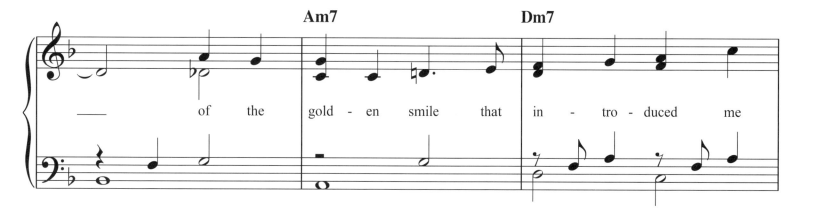

_____ of the   gold - en smile that   in - tro - duced me

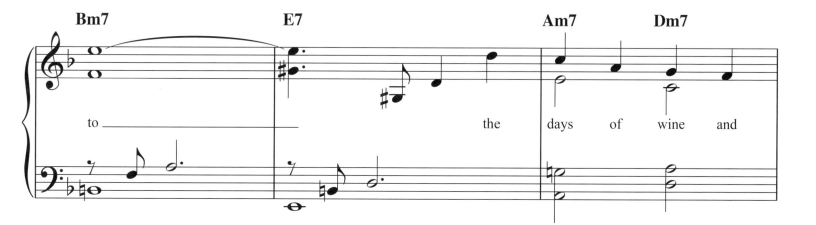

to _____   the   days   of   wine   and

ros - es   and   you.   rit.

CRISTOFORI'S DREAM

By DAVID LANZ

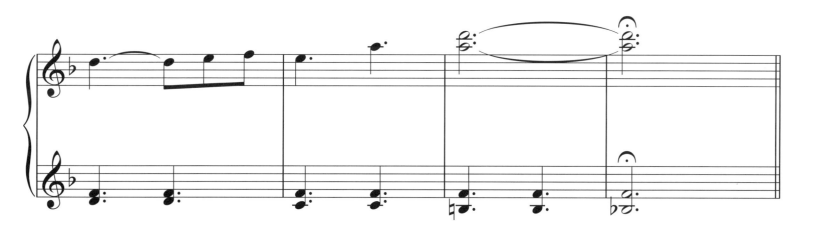

L.H. loco on repeat

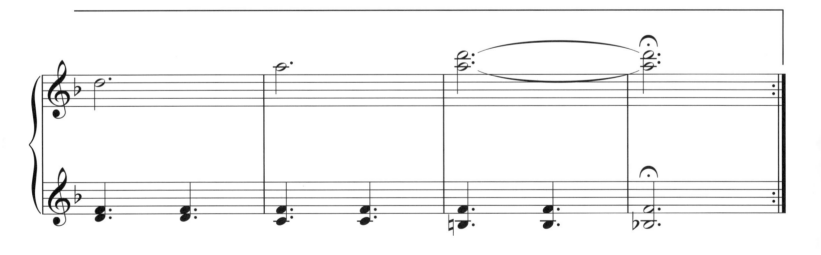

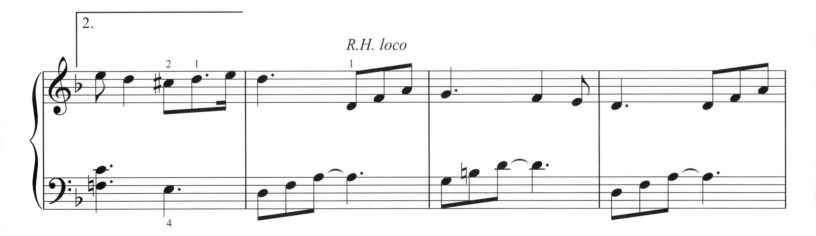

cresc.

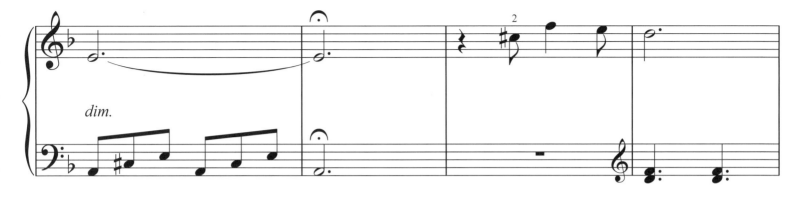

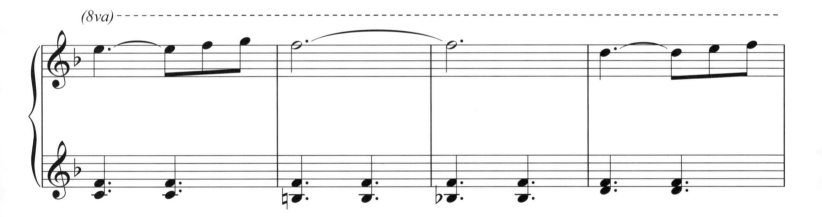

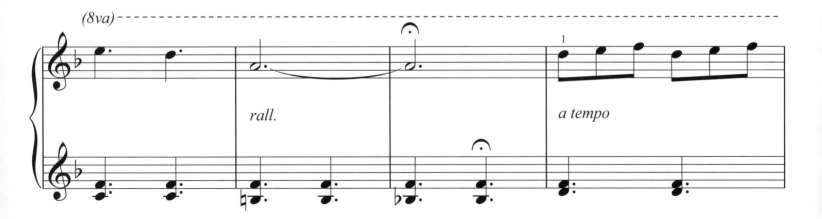

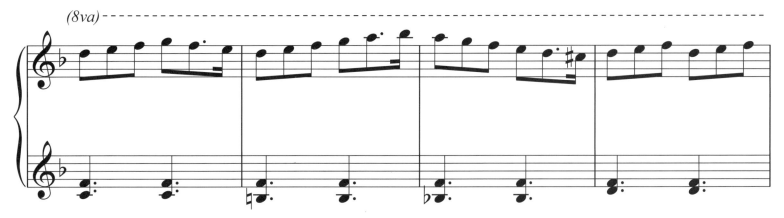

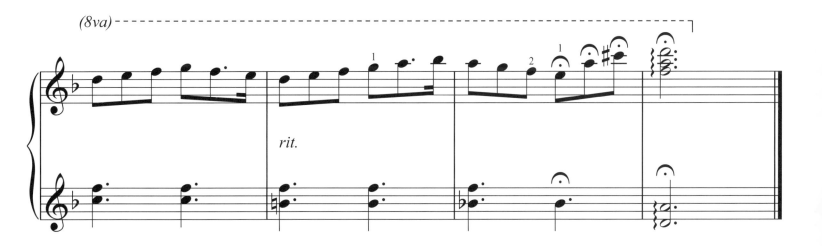

DAWN
from PRIDE & PREJUDICE

By DARIO MARIANELLI

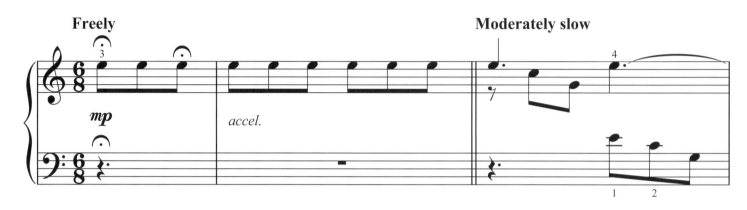

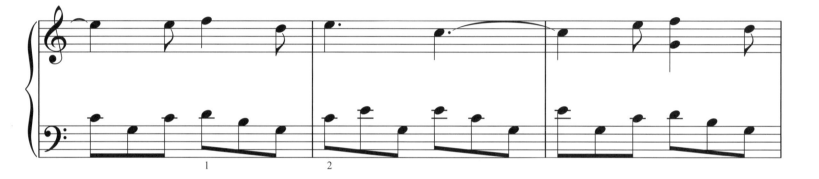

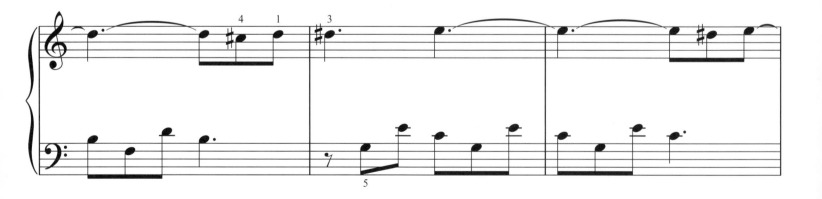

Moderately fast

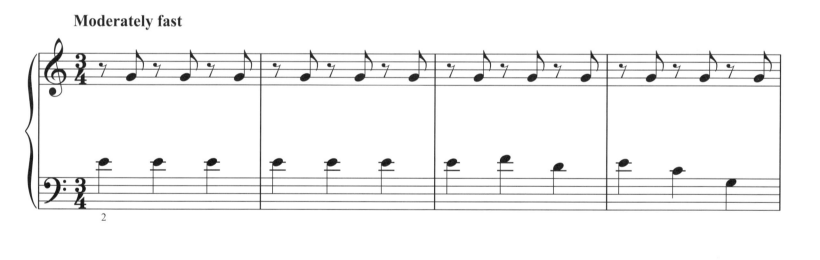

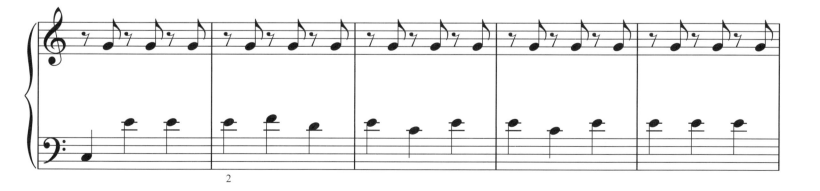

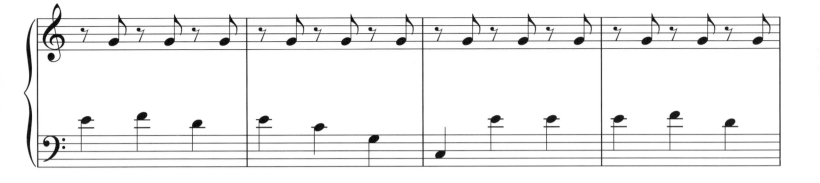

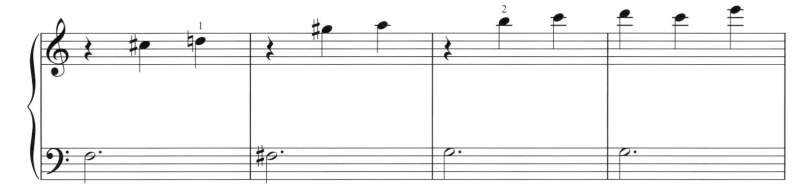

Slightly slower

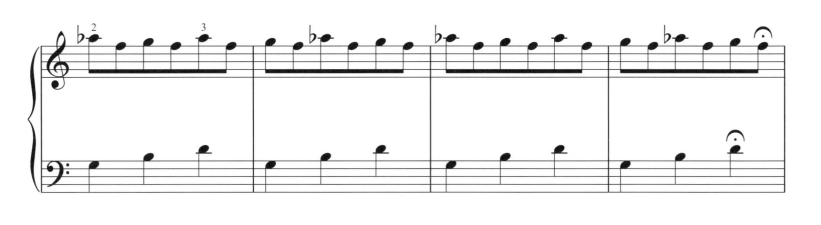

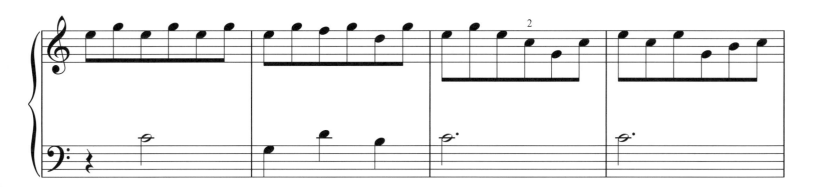

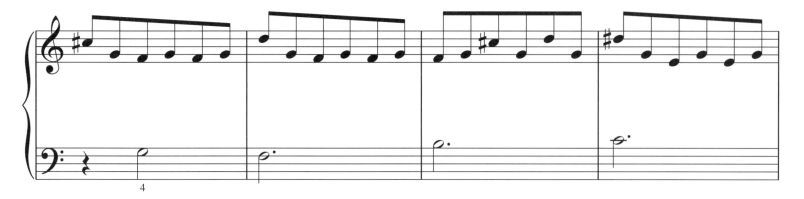

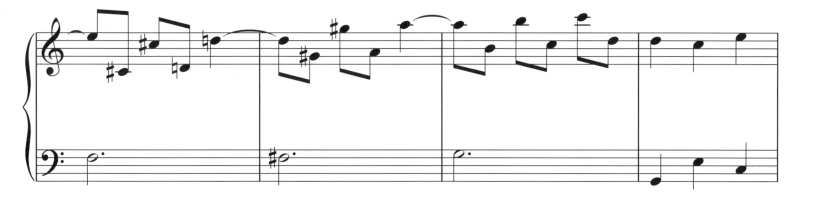

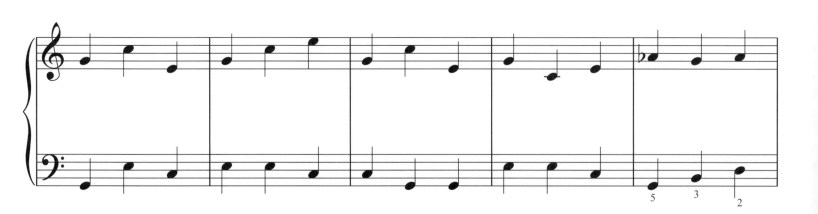

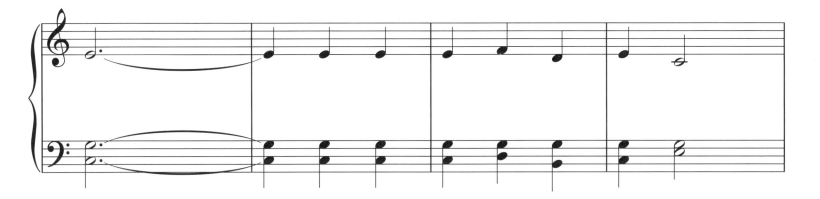

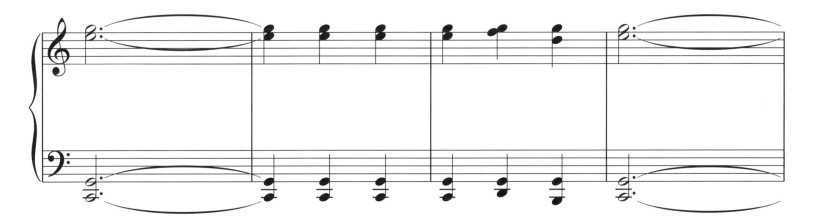

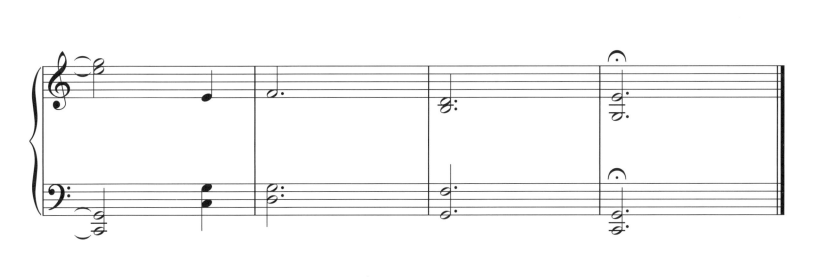

FIELDS OF GOLD

Music and Lyrics by
STING

Flowing, moderately

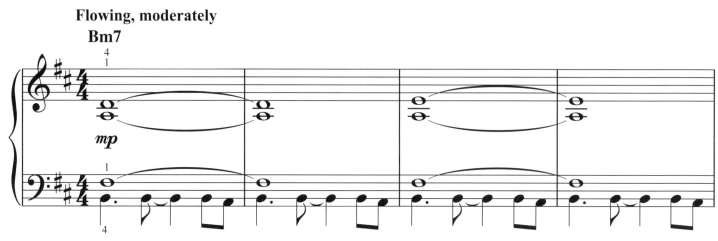

You'll re-

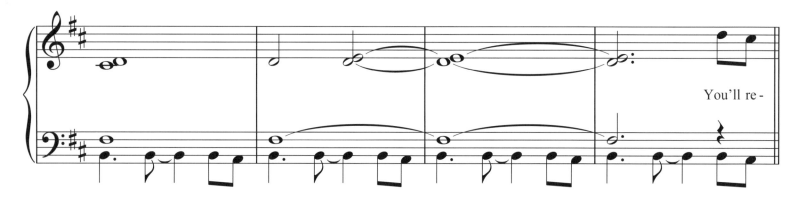

mem - ber me ____ when the west wind moves ____ up - on the fields ____ of
stay with me, ____ will you be my love ____ a - mong the fields ____ of

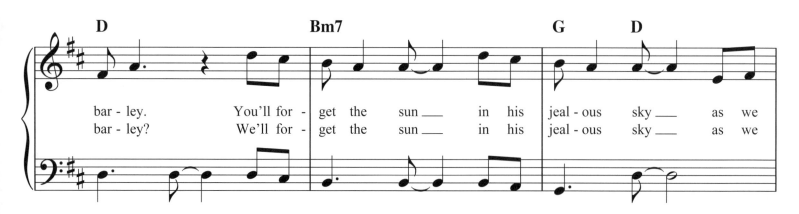

bar - ley. You'll for - get the sun ____ in his jeal - ous sky ____ as we
bar - ley? We'll for - get the sun ____ in his jeal - ous sky ____ as we

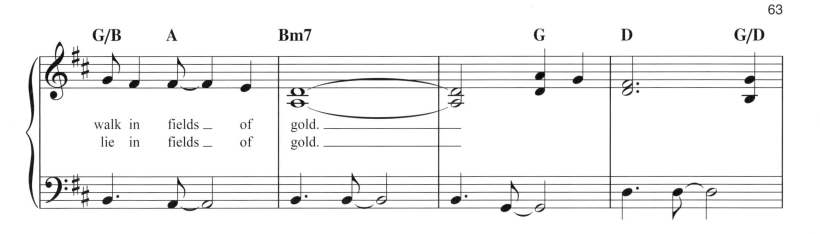

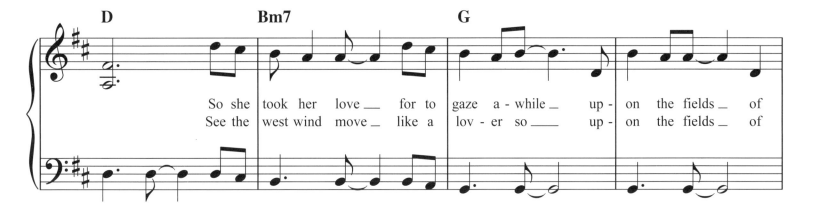

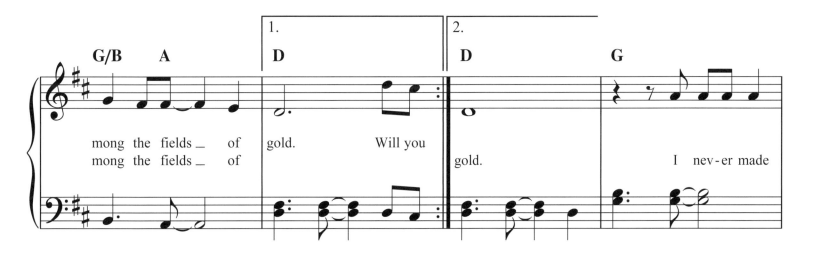

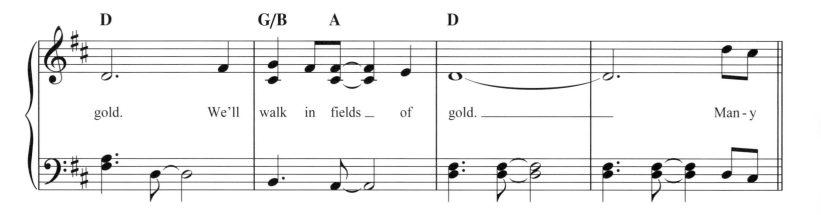

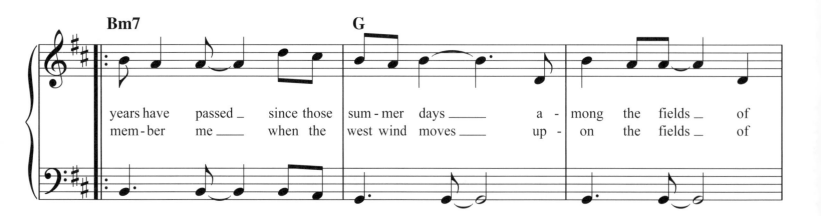

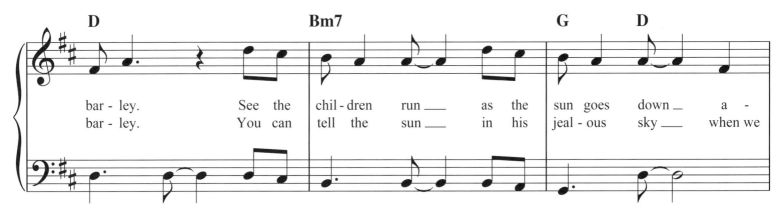

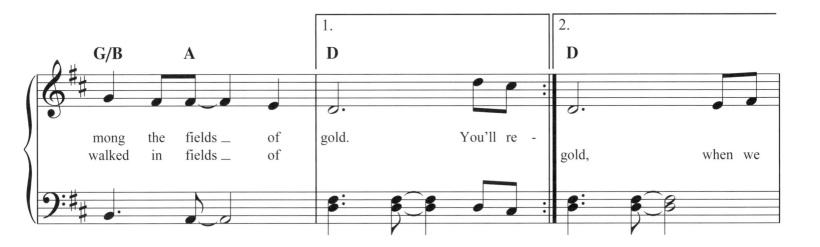

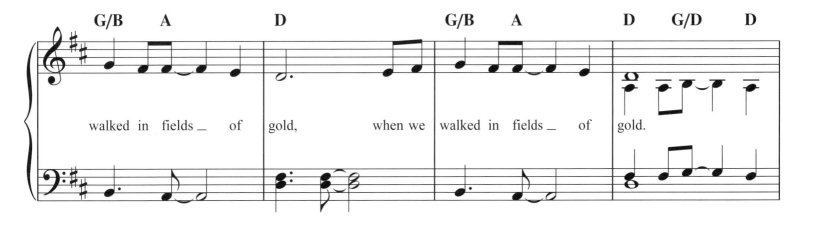

GABRIEL'S OBOE
from the Motion Picture THE MISSION

Music by
ENNIO MORRICONE

Slowly, expressively

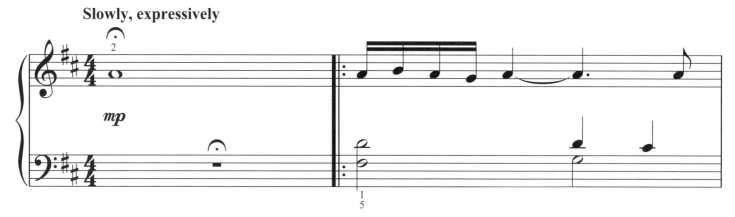

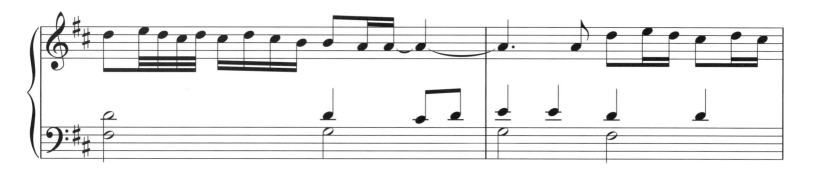

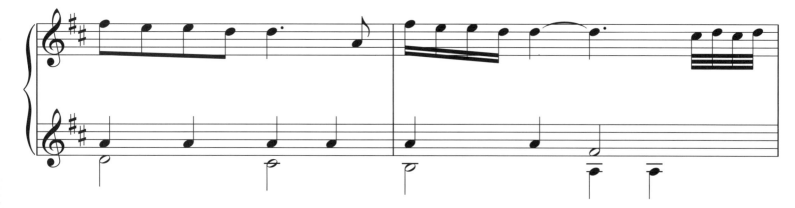

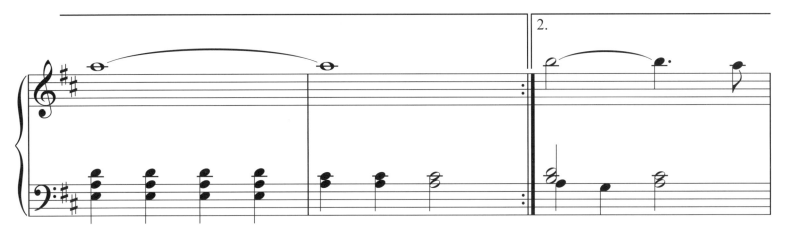

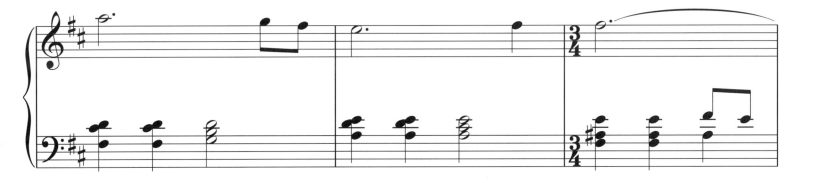

THEME FROM ICE CASTLES

(Through the Eyes of Love)
from ICE CASTLES

Music by MARVIN HAMLISCH
Lyrics by CAROLE BAYER SAGER

Slowly, with feeling

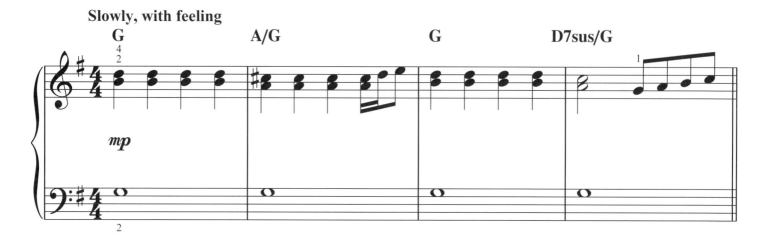

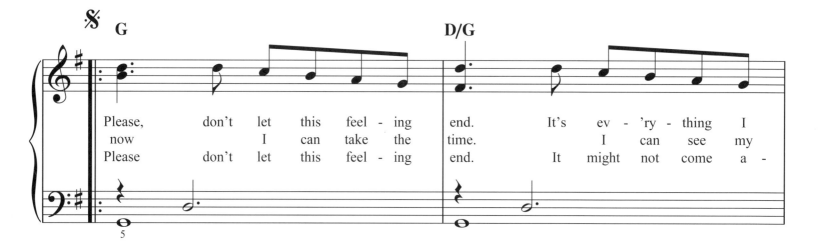

Please, don't let this feel - ing end. It's ev - 'ry - thing I
now I can take the time. I can see my
Please don't let this feel - ing end. It might not come a -

am, ev - 'ry - thing I want to be.
life as it comes up shin - ing now.
gain and I want to re - mem - ber

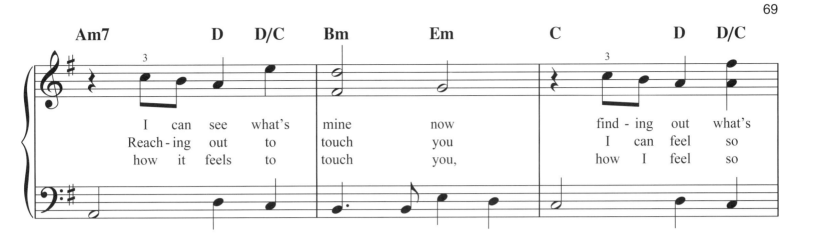

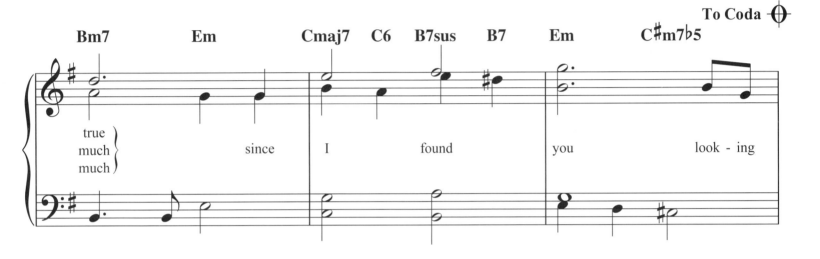

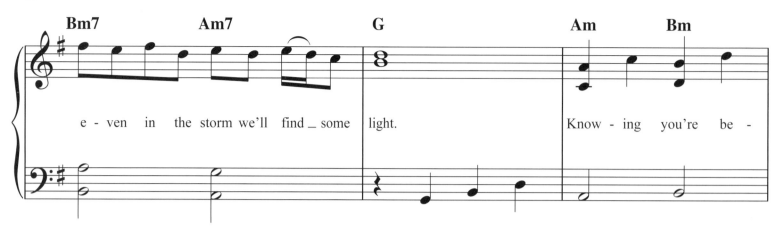

e - ven in the storm we'll find _ some light.

Know - ing you're be -

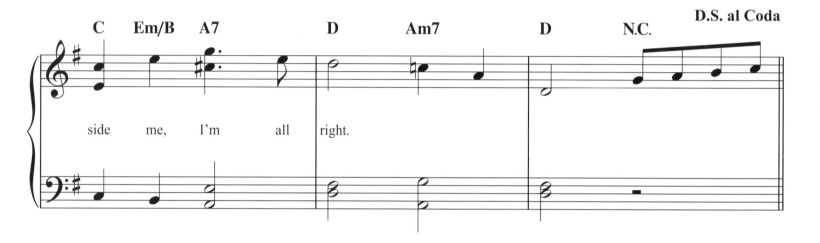

side me, I'm all right.

through the eyes ___ of love.

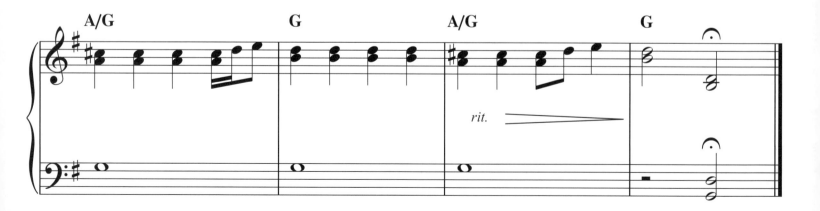

IMAGINE

Words and Music by
JOHN LENNON

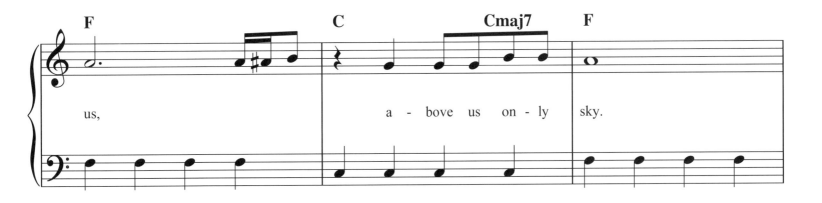

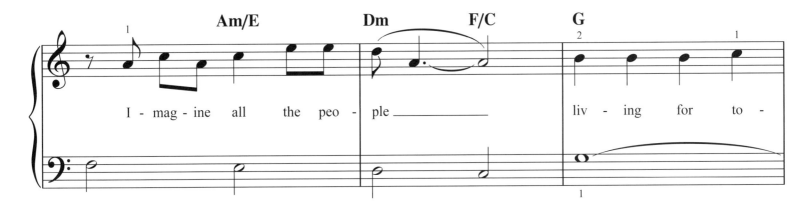

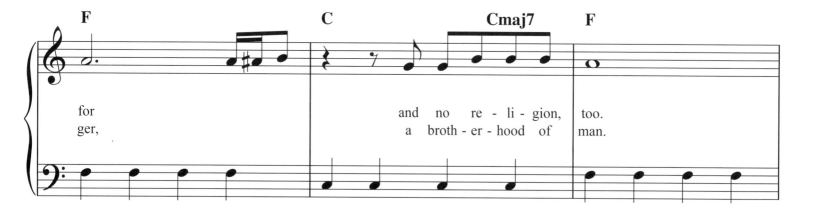

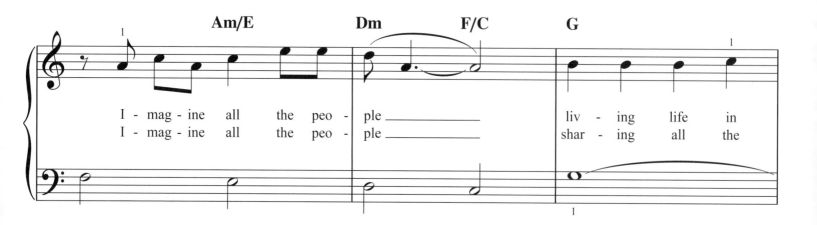

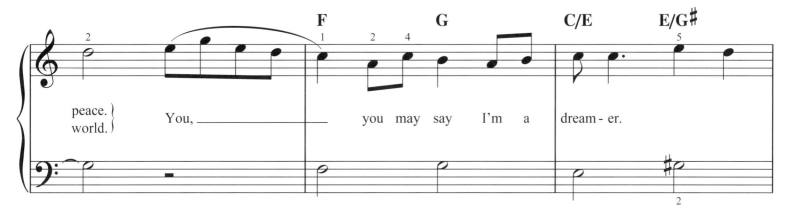

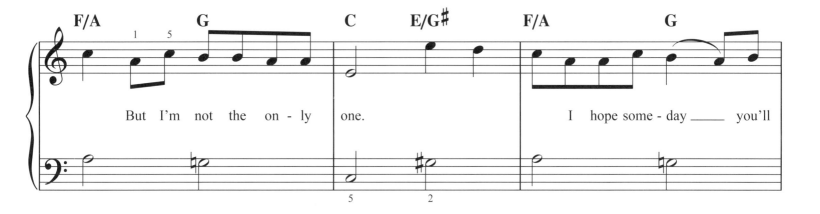

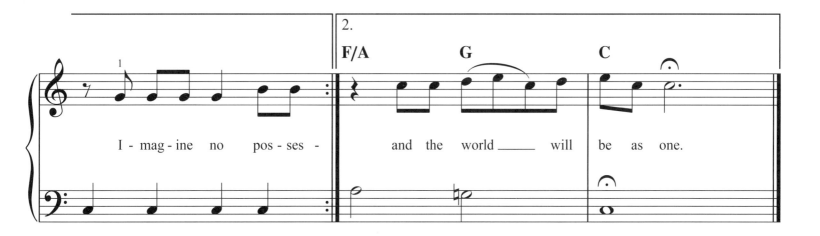

JESSICA'S THEME
(Breaking In the Colt)

By BRUCE ROWLAND

With motion

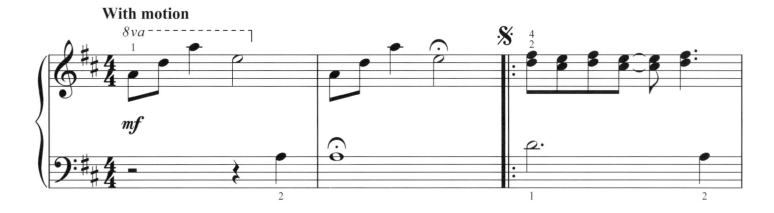

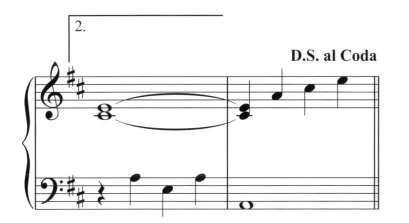

IN A SENTIMENTAL MOOD

Words and Music by DUKE ELLINGTON,
IRVING MILLS and MANNY KURTZ

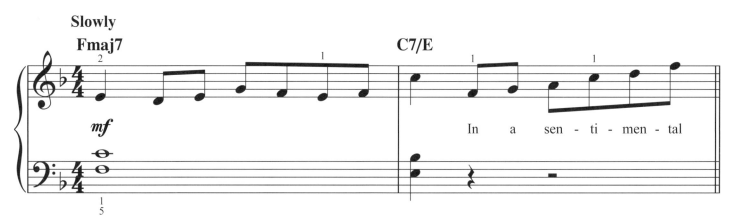

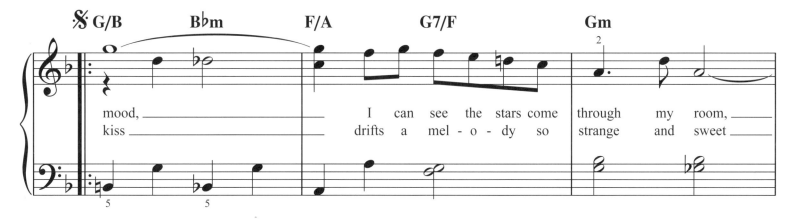

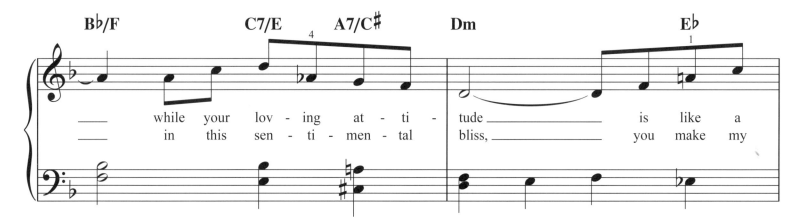

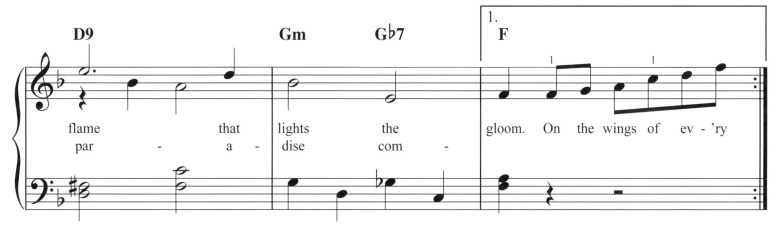

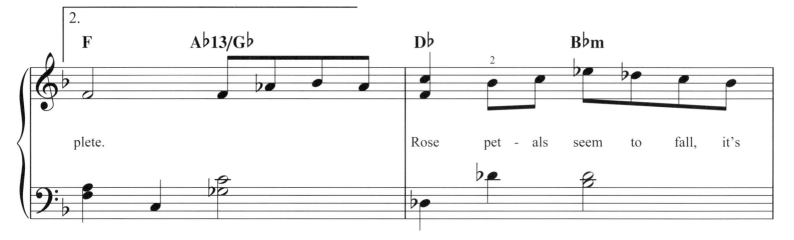

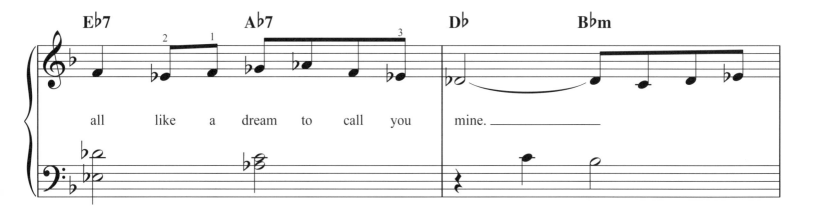

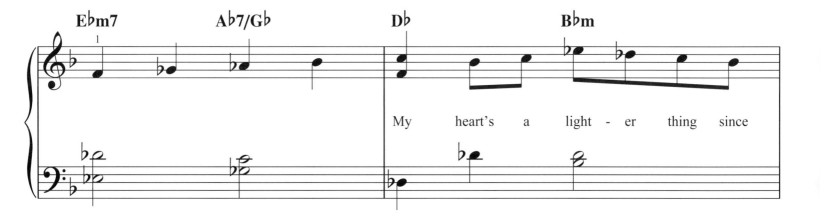

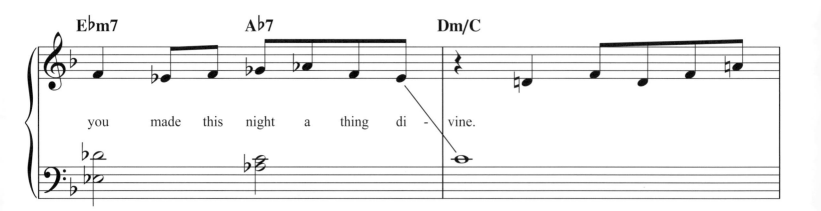

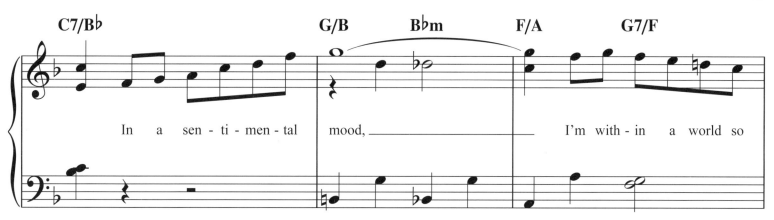

In a sen - ti - men - tal mood, _____ I'm with - in a world so

heav - en - ly, _____ for I nev - er dreamt that you'd _____ be lov - ing

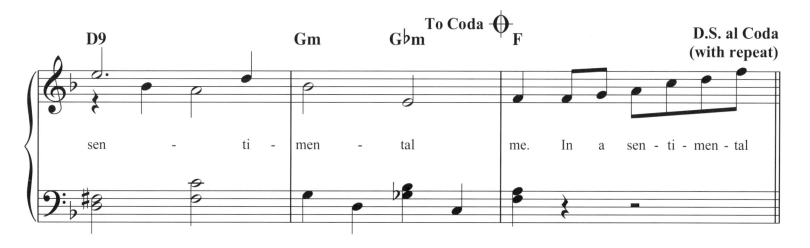

sen - ti - men - tal me. In a sen - ti - men - tal

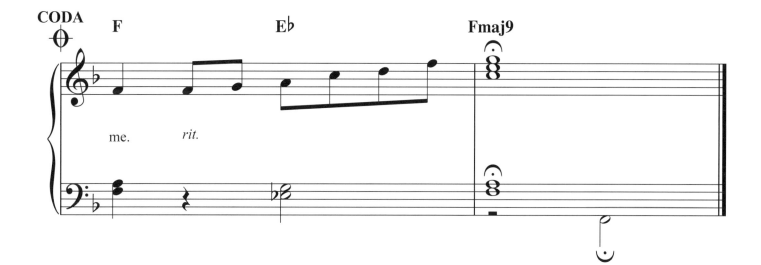

me. *rit.*

MAKE YOU FEEL MY LOVE

Words and Music by
BOB DYLAN

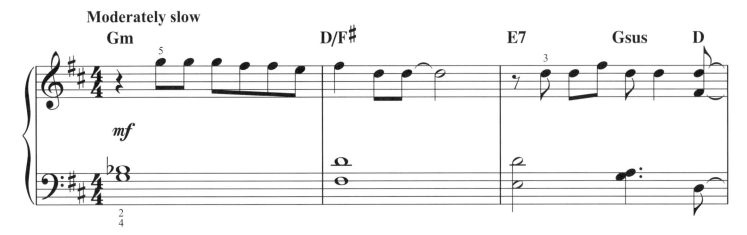

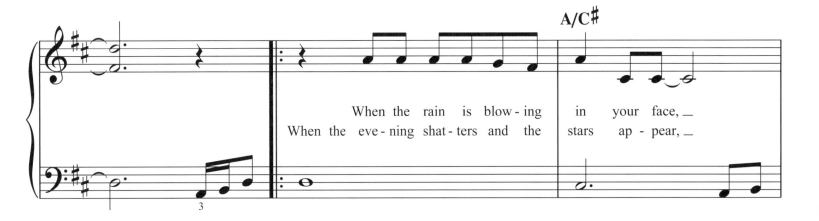

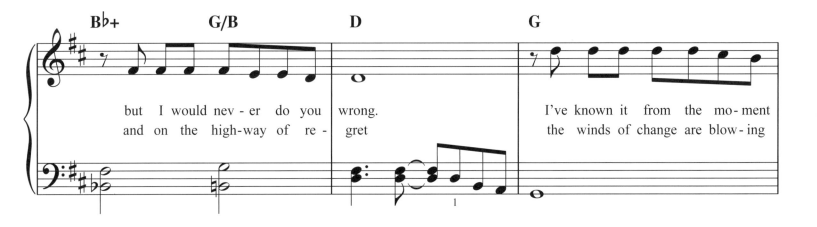

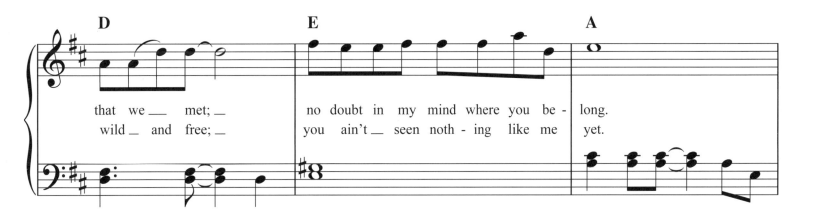

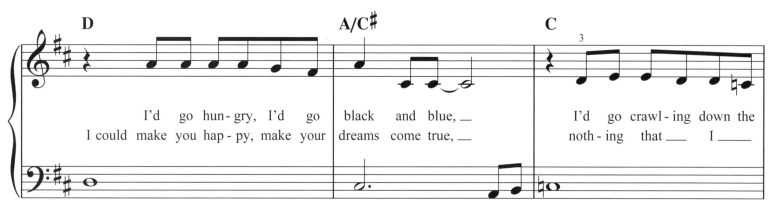

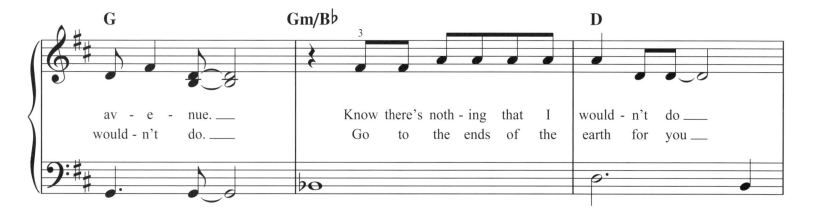

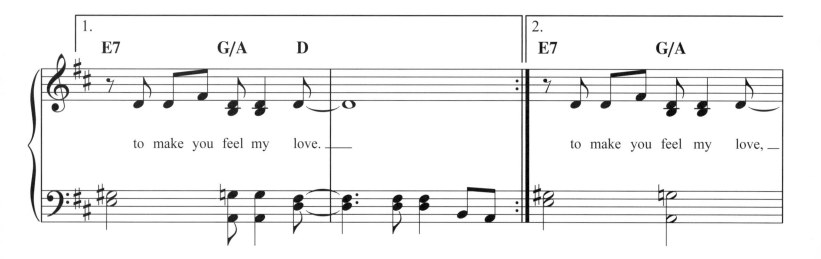

LONGER

Words and Music by
DAN FOGELBERG

Moderately

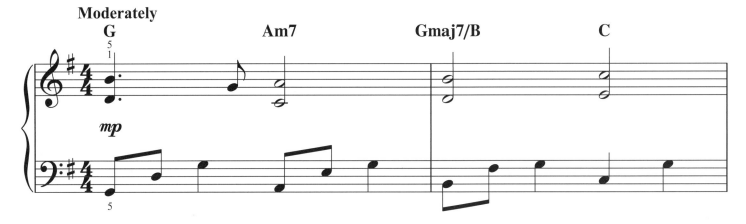

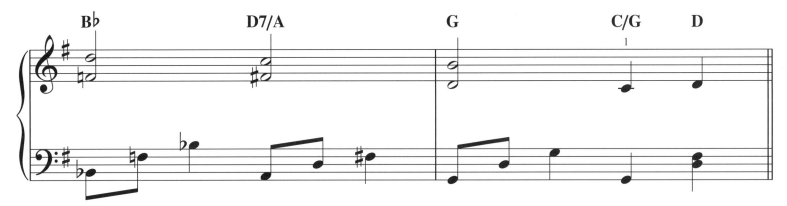

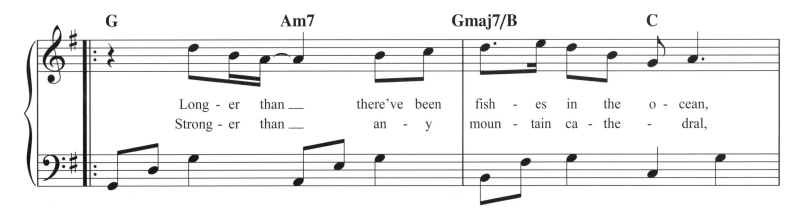

Long-er than ___ there've been fish-es in the o-cean,

Strong-er than ___ an-y moun-tain ca-the- -dral,

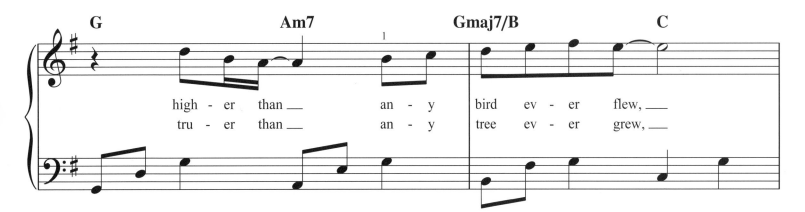

high-er than ___ an-y bird ev-er flew, ___

tru-er than ___ an-y tree ev-er grew, ___

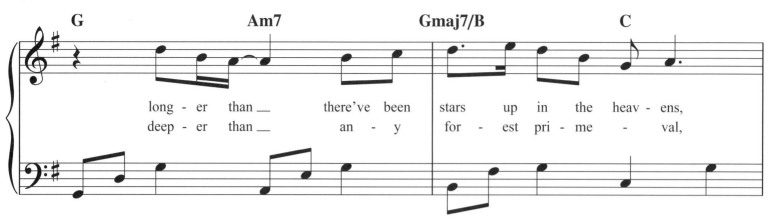

G   Am7   Gmaj7/B   C

long - er than ___ there've been stars up in the heav - ens,
deep - er than ___ an - y for - est pri - me - val,

Bb   D7/A   1.   G   C/G   D   2.   G

I've been in love __ with you. ____
I am in love __ with you. ____

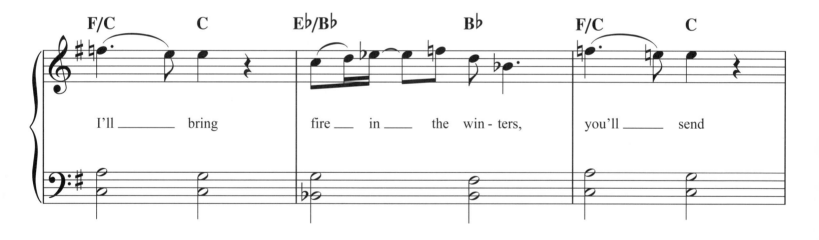

F/C   C   Eb/Bb   Bb   F/C   C

I'll ____ bring   fire __ in __ the win - ters,   you'll ____ send

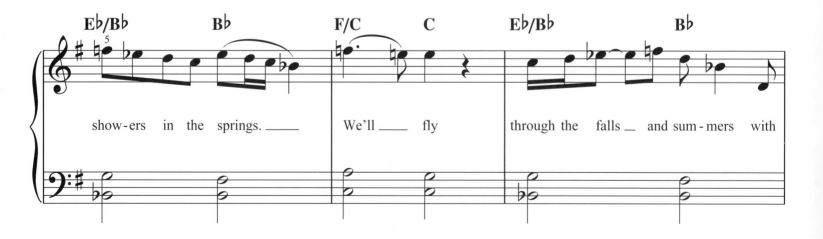

Eb/Bb   Bb   F/C   C   Eb/Bb   Bb

show - ers in the springs. ____   We'll ____ fly   through the falls __ and sum - mers with

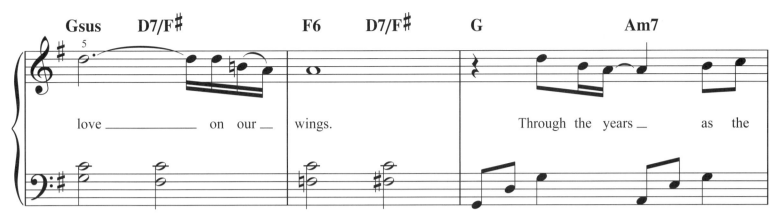

love _____ on our _ wings. Through the years _ as the

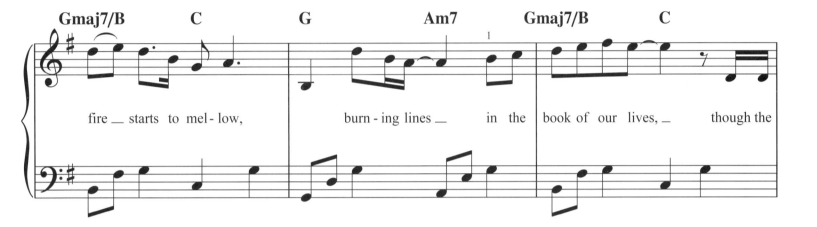

fire _ starts to mel - low, burn - ing lines _ in the book of our lives, _ though the

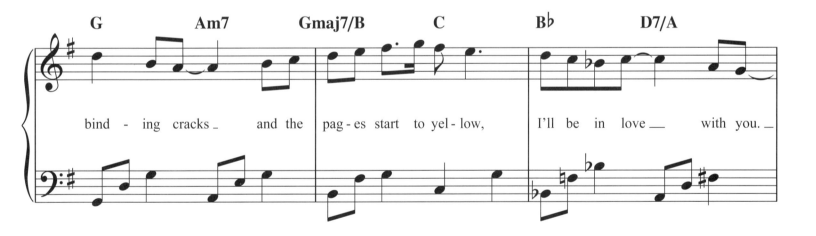

bind - ing cracks _ and the pag - es start to yel - low, I'll be in love _ with you. _

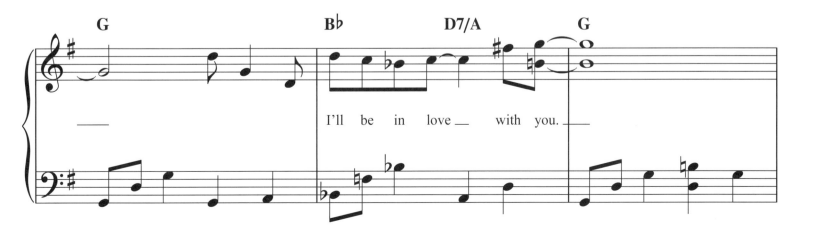

_ I'll be in love _ with you. _

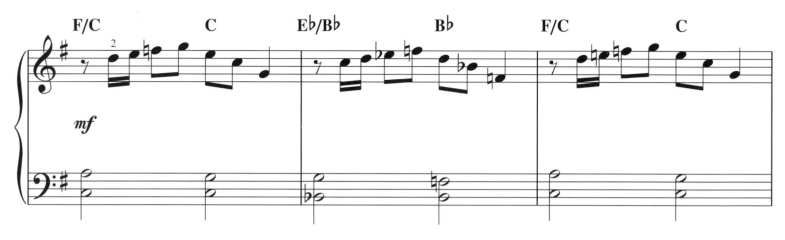

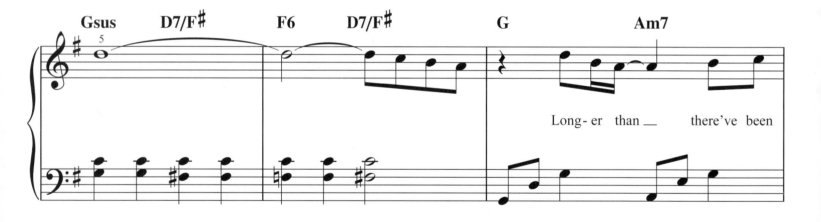

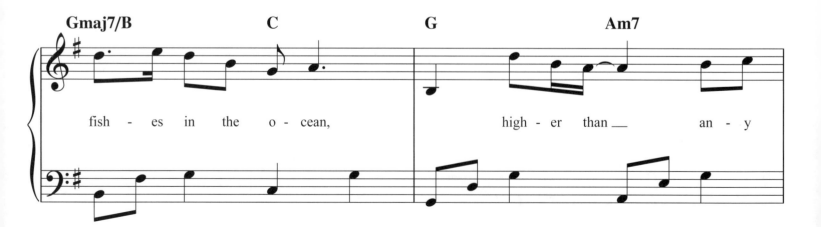

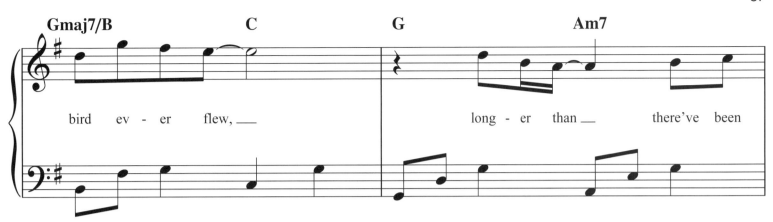

bird ev - er flew, ___ long - er than ___ there've been

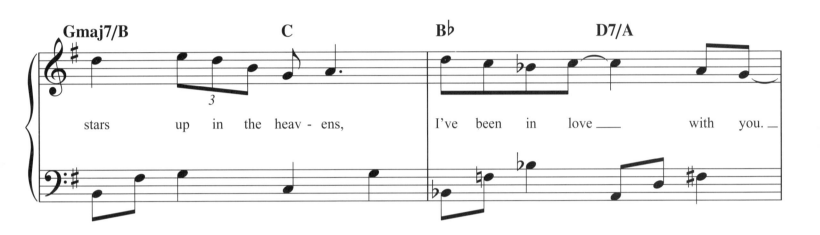

stars up in the heav - ens, I've been in love ___ with you. ___

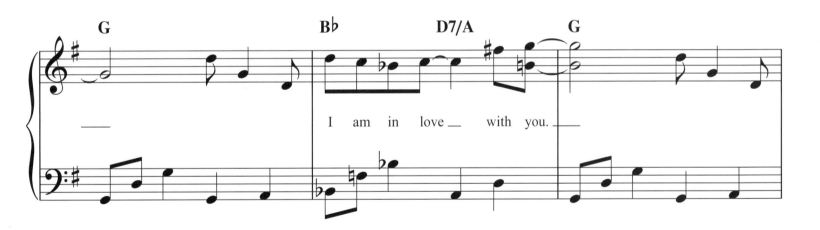

___ I am in love ___ with you. ___

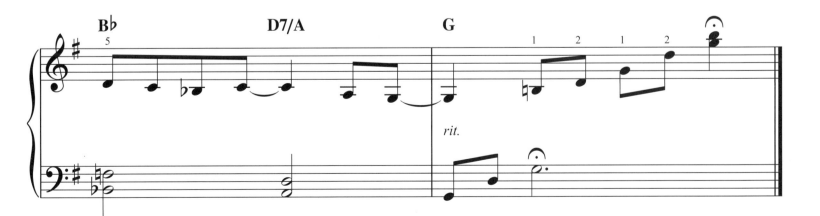

rit.

MIA & SEBASTIAN'S THEME

from LA LA LAND

Music by
JUSTIN HURWITZ

Moderately slow, expressively

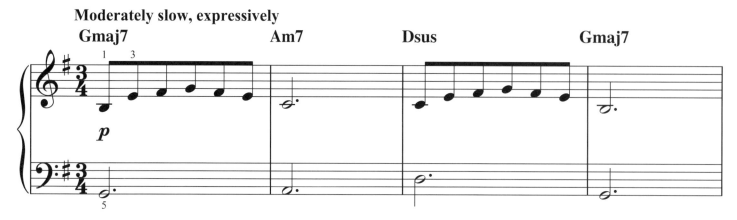

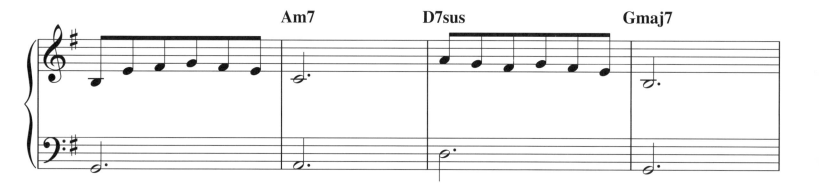

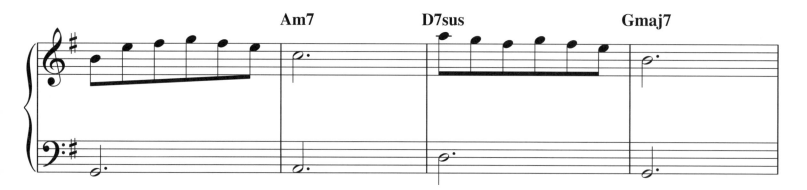

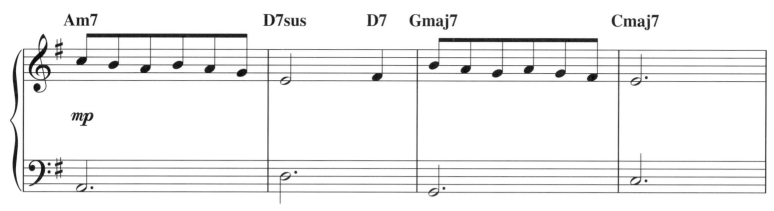

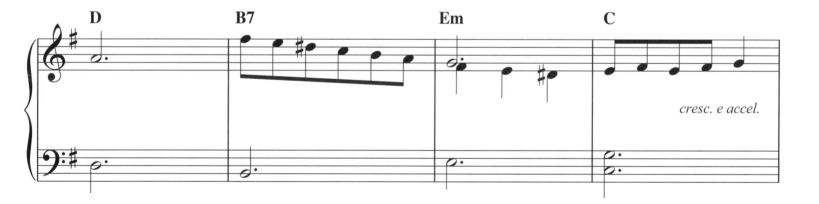

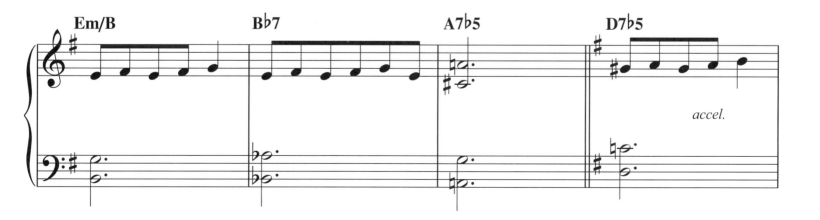

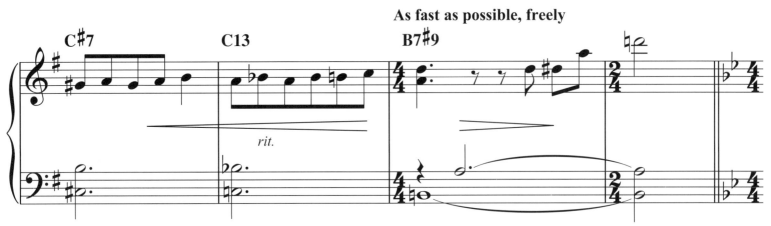

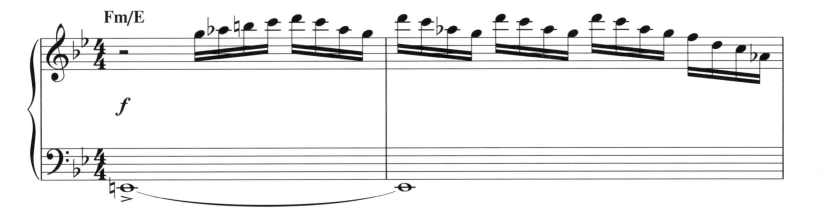

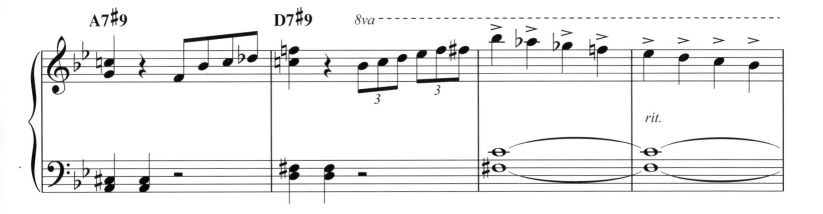

MUSIC BOX DANCER

Composed by
FRANK MILLS

Bright and lively

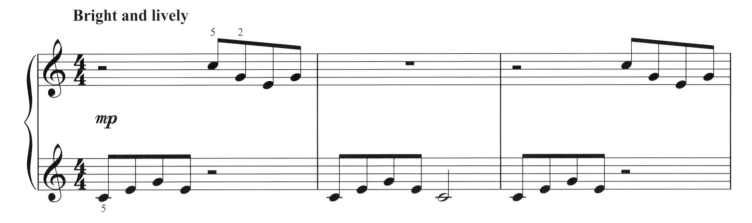

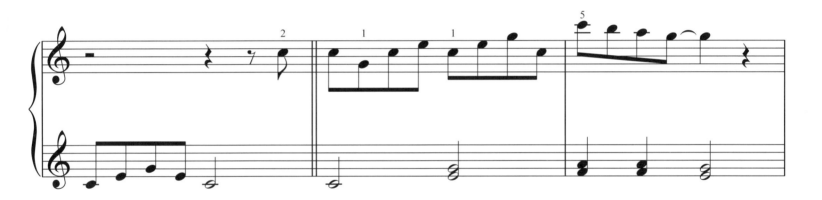

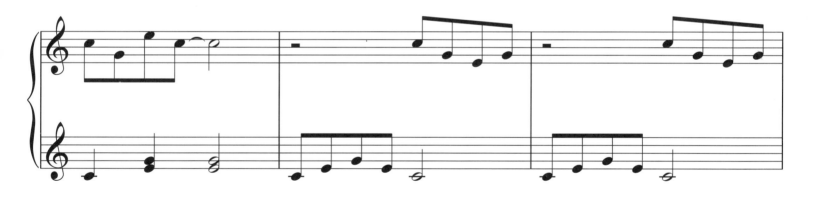

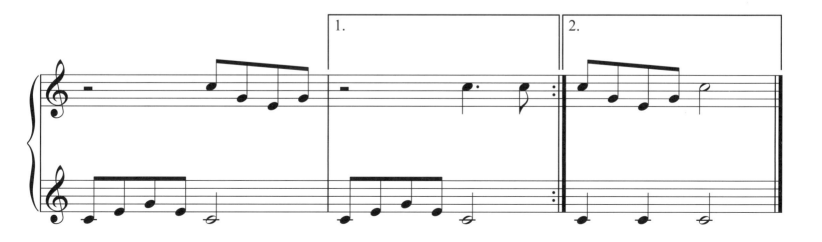

THE MUSIC OF GOODBYE
from OUT OF AFRICA

Words and Music by JOHN BARRY,
ALAN BERGMAN and MARILYN BERGMAN

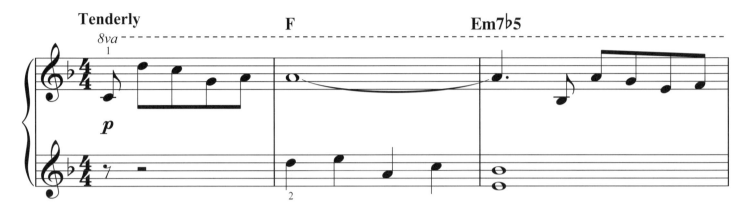

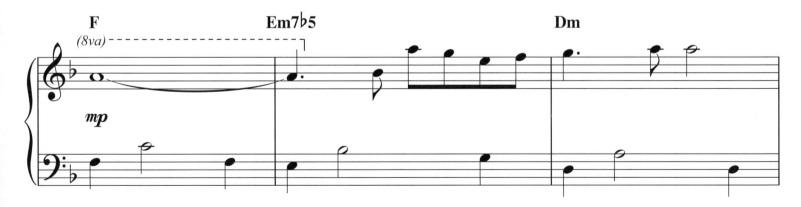

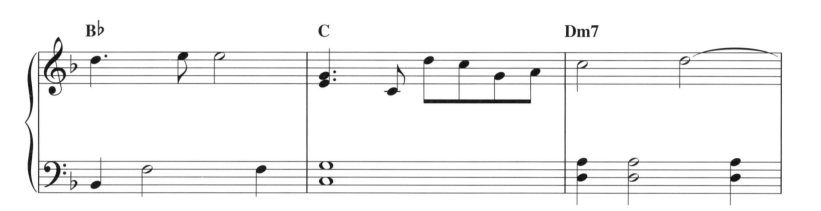

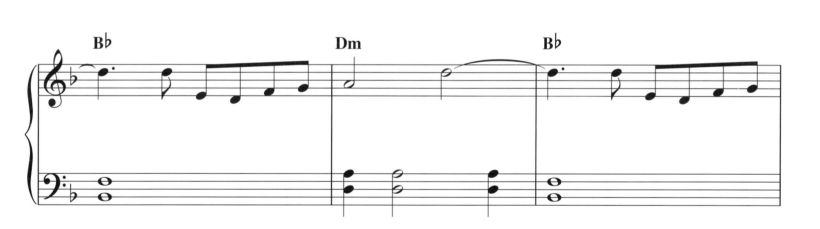

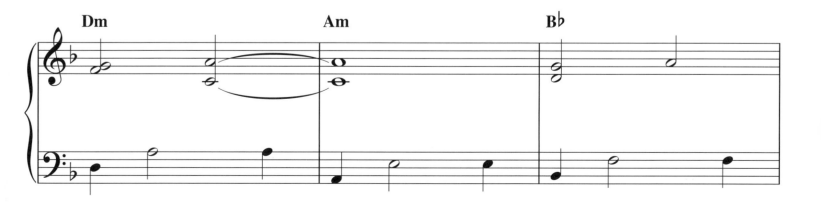

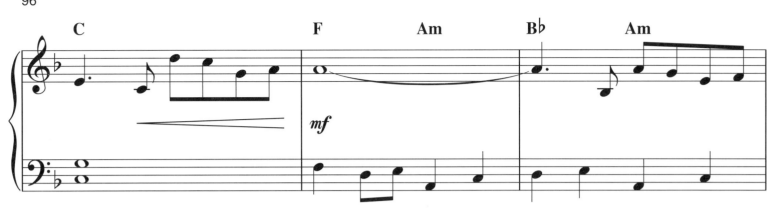

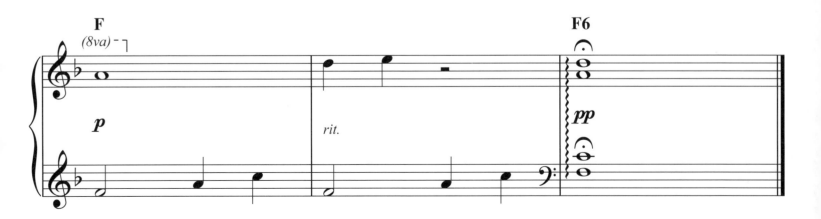

OVER THE RAINBOW
from THE WIZARD OF OZ

Music by HAROLD ARLEN
Lyric by E.Y. "YIP" HARBURG

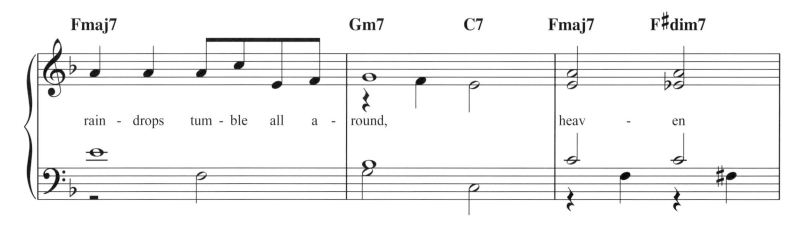

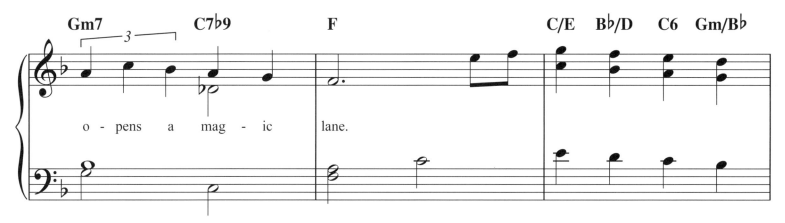

When all the clouds dark-en up the sky-way, there's a rain-bow high-way to be

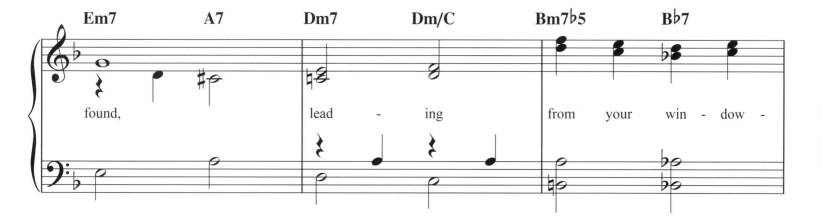

found, lead - ing from your win - dow -

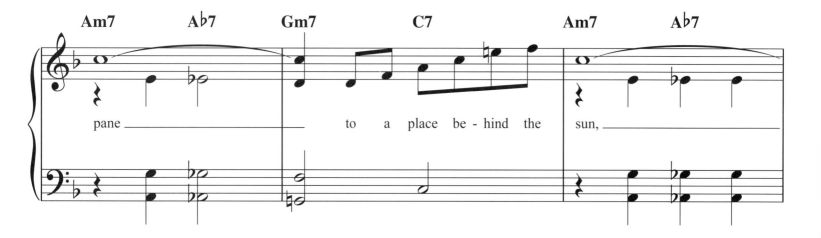

pane _____ to a place be-hind the sun, _____

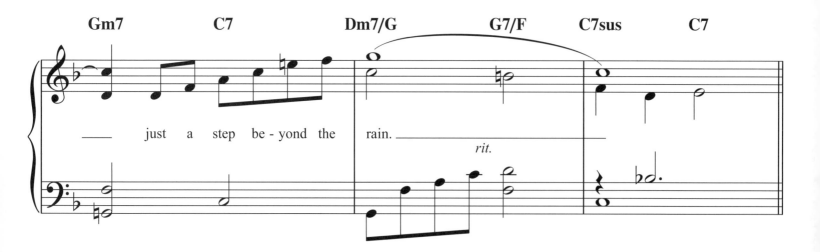

_____ just a step be-yond the rain. _____ *rit.*

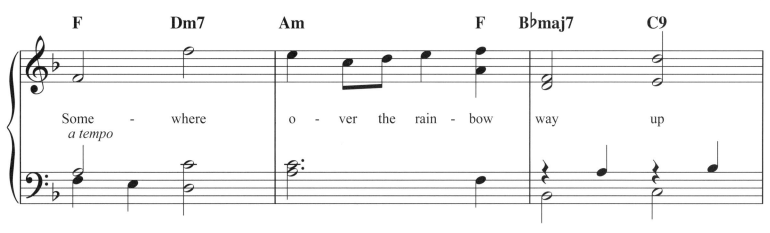

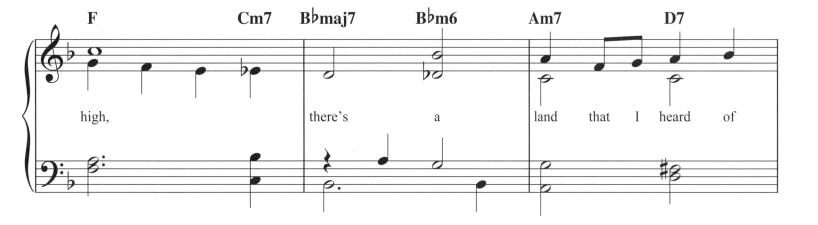

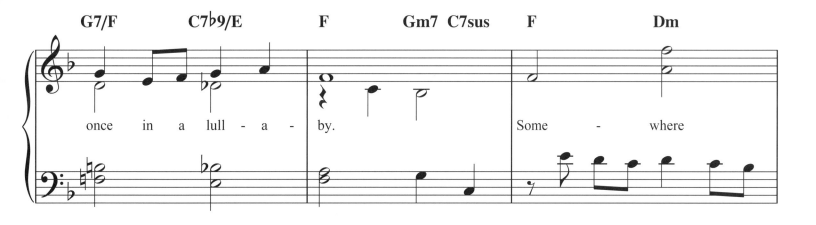

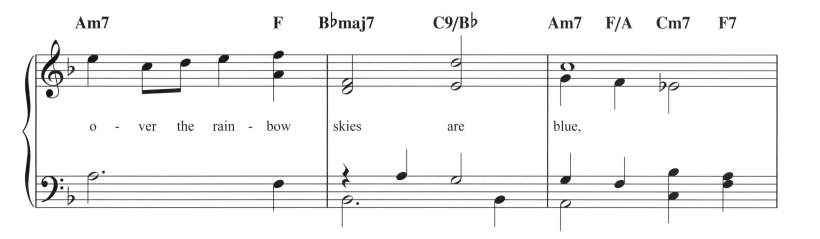

and the dreams that you dare to dream real - ly do come

true. _____ Some - day I'll wish up - on a star and wake up where the clouds are far be -

hind me. Where trou - bles melt like lem - on drops, a -

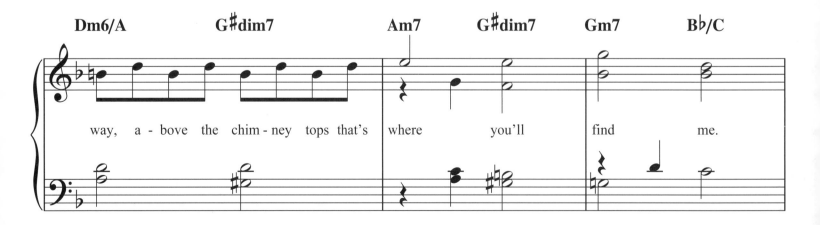

way, a - bove the chim - ney tops that's where you'll find me.

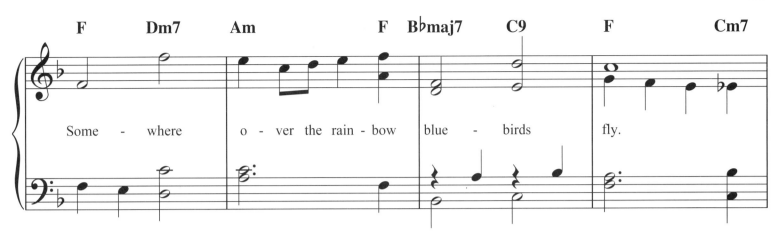

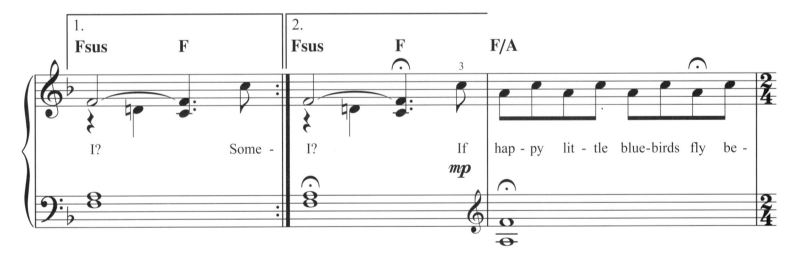

MY HEART WILL GO ON

(Love Theme from 'Titanic')

from the Paramount and Twentieth Century Fox Motion Picture TITANIC

Music by JAMES HORNER
Lyric by WILL JENNINGS

Moderately

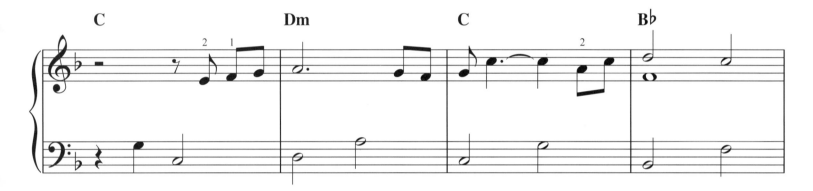

Ev - 'ry night in my dreams I see you, I

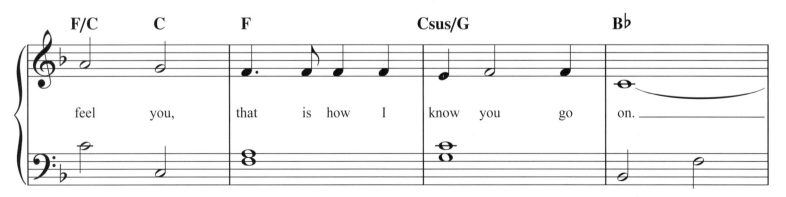

feel you, that is how I know you go on.

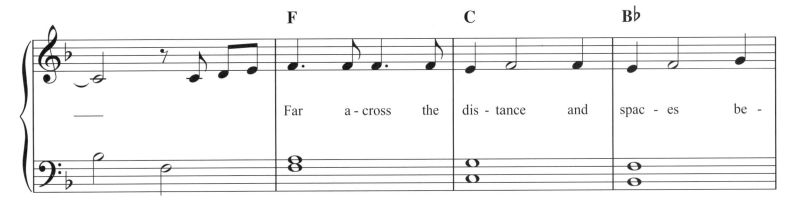

Far a - cross the dis - tance and spac - es be -

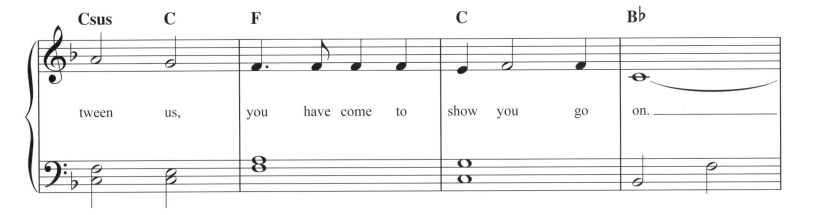

tween us, you have come to show you go on. _____

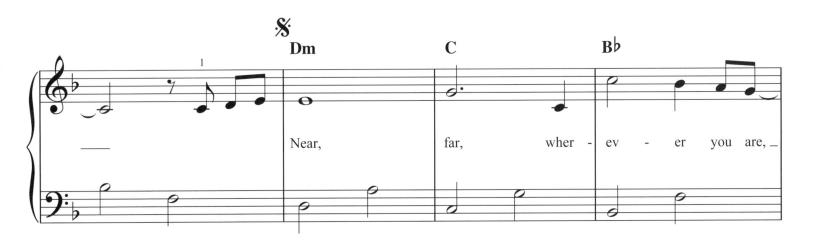

Near, far, wher - ev - er you are, _

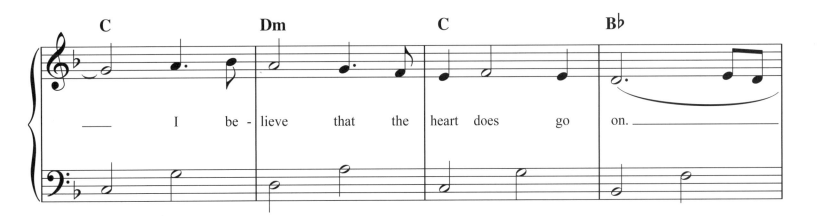

_____ I be - lieve that the heart does go on. _____

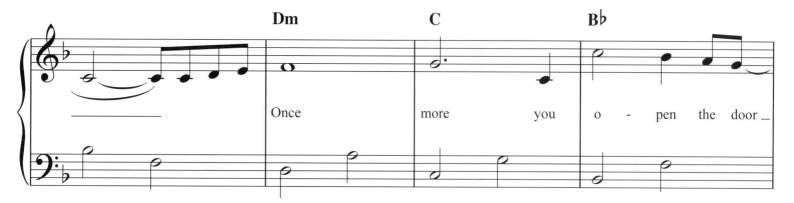

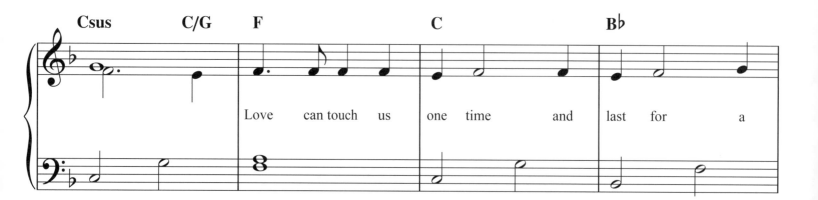

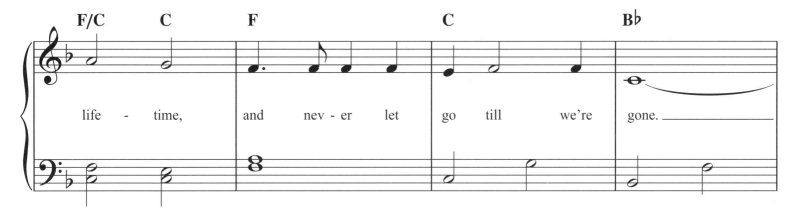

life - time, and nev - er let go till we're gone. ___

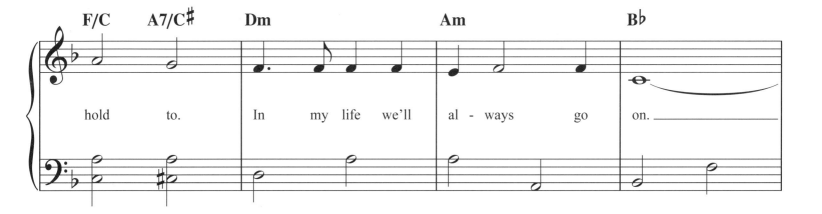

___ Love was when I loved you; one true time I

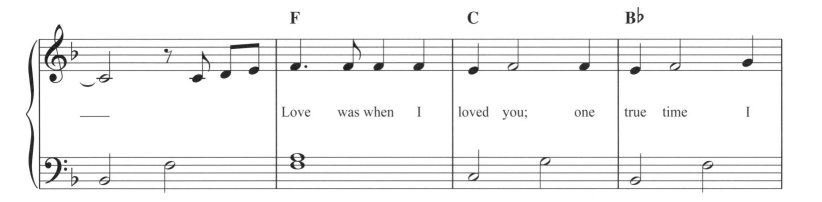

hold to. In my life we'll al - ways go on. ___

D.S. al Coda

CODA

on.

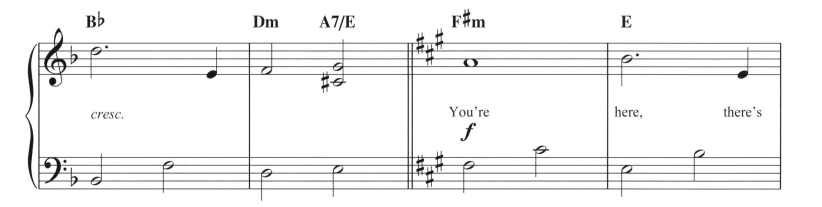

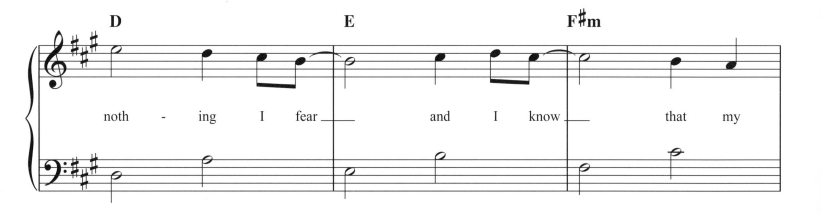

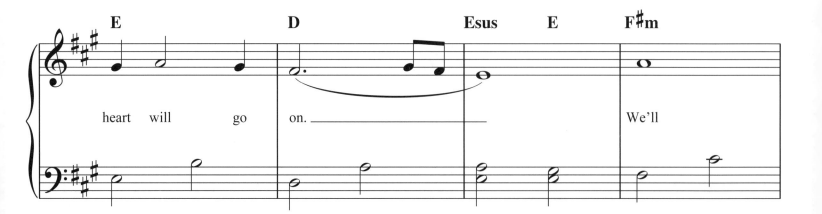

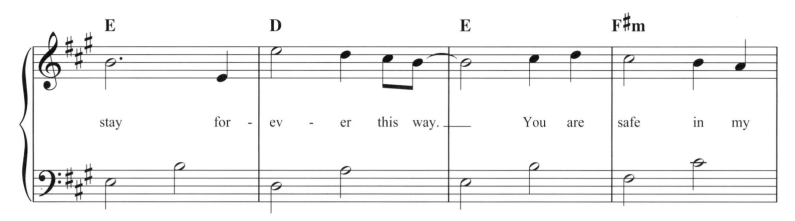

stay   for - ev - er this way.___   You are safe in my

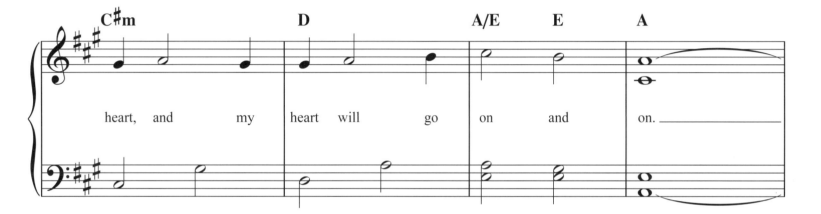

heart, and   my   heart will   go   on   and   on.___

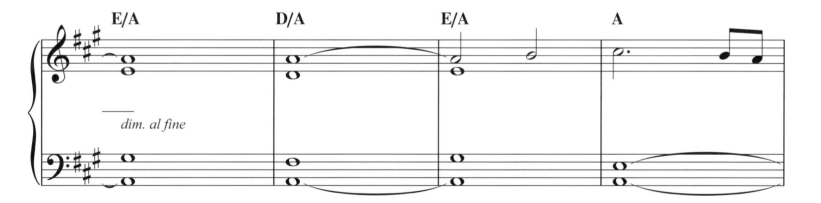

dim. al fine

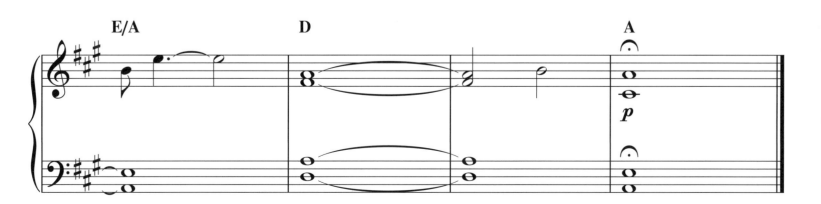

p

NEW YORK STATE OF MIND

Words and Music by
BILLY JOEL

Some folks like to get a - way, take a
I seen all the mov - ie stars in their
Comes down to re - al - i - ty and it's

hol - i - day from the neigh - bor - hood, hop a flight to
fan - cy cars and their lim - ou - sines, been high in the
fine with me, 'cause I've let it slide. Don't care if it's

Mi - am - i Beach or to Hol - ly - wood.
Rock - ies un - der the ev - er - greens.
Chi - na - town or on Riv - er - side.

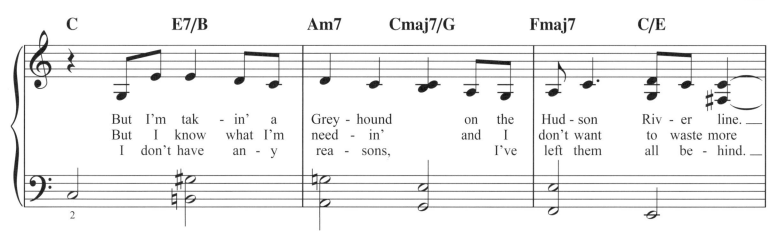

C   E7/B   Am7   Cmaj7/G   Fmaj7   C/E

But I'm tak - in' a Grey - hound   on the Hud - son Riv - er line. ___
But I know what I'm need - in', and I don't want to waste more
I don't have an - y rea - sons, I've left them all be - hind. ___

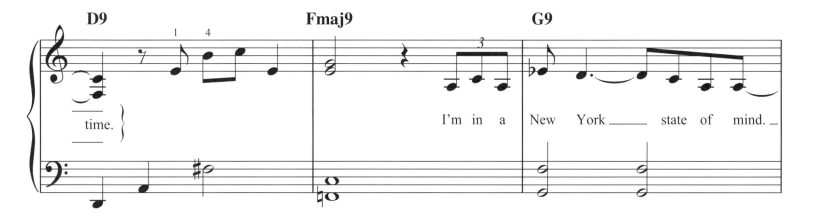

D9   Fmaj9   G9

time.   I'm in a New York ___ state of mind. ___

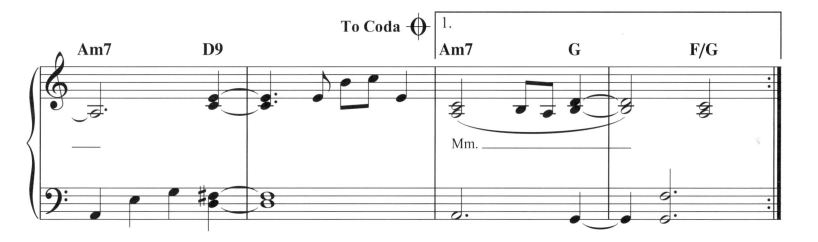

Am7   D9   **To Coda** ⊕   1.   Am7   G   F/G

Mm. ___

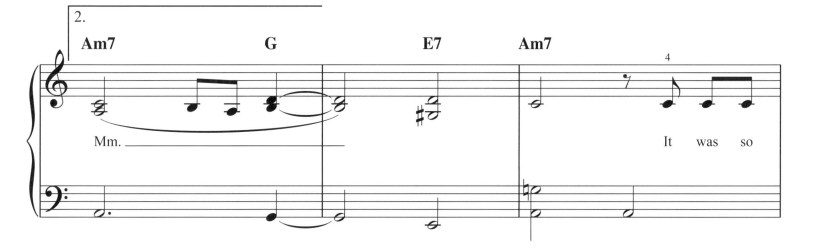

2.   Am7   G   E7   Am7

Mm. ___   It was so

eas - y liv - in' day by day, out of touch

with the rhy-thm and blues. But now I need

a lit - tle give and take the New York Times,

D.S. al Coda

the Dai - ly News.

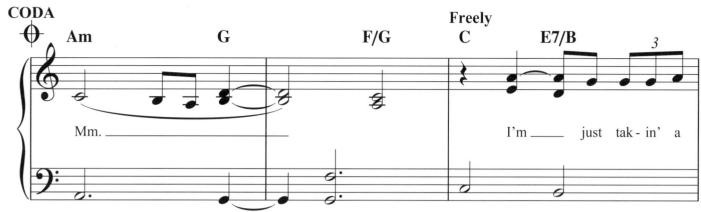

CODA

Mm. _____

I'm _____ just tak - in' a

Grey - hound on the Hud - son Riv - er line.

I'm in a

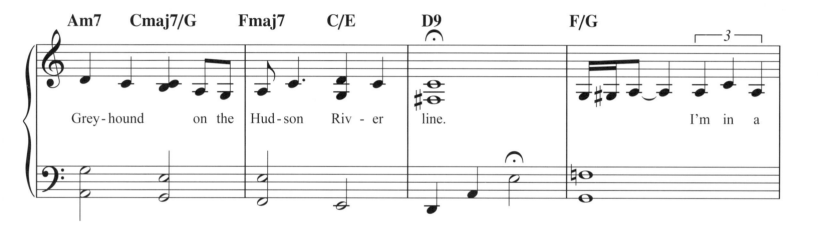

New York state of mind. _____

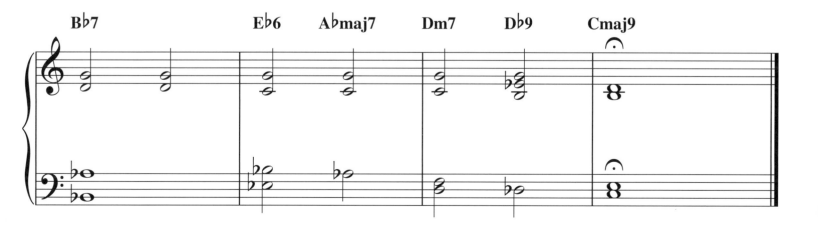

ON GOLDEN POND
Main Theme from ON GOLDEN POND

Music by DAVE GRUSIN

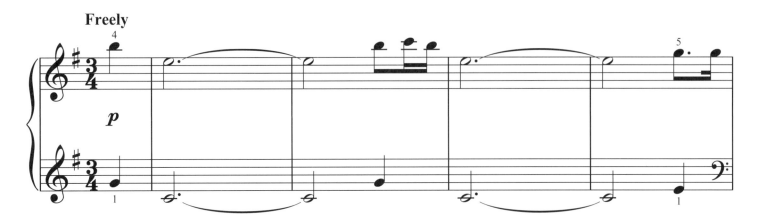

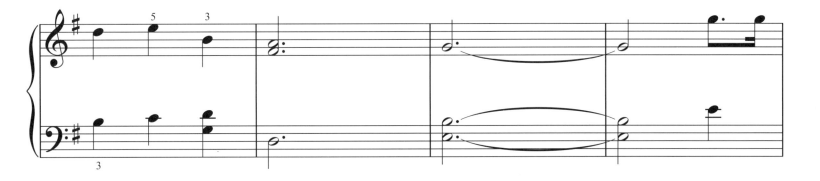

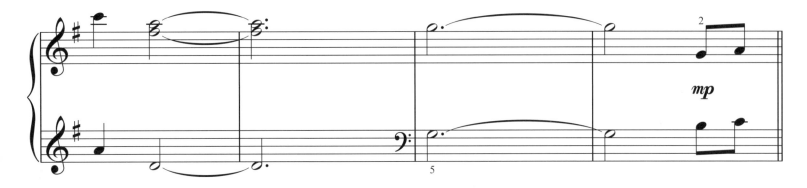

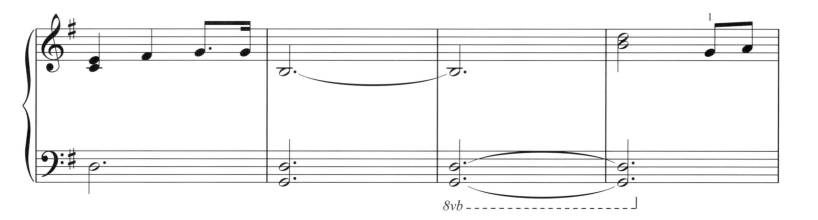

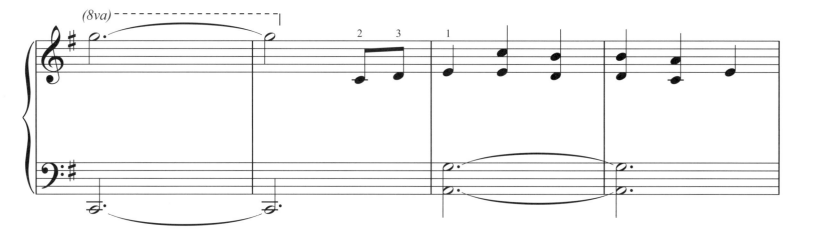

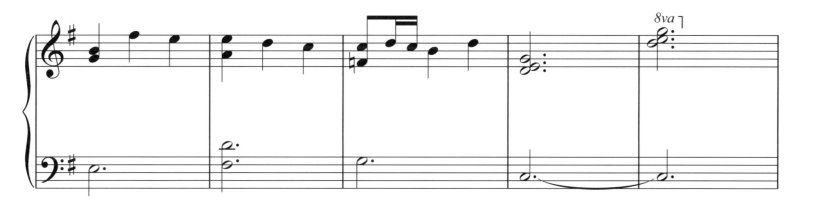

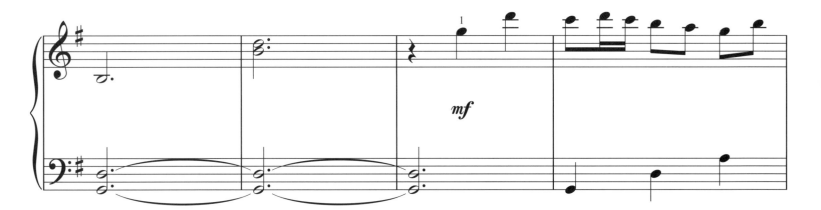

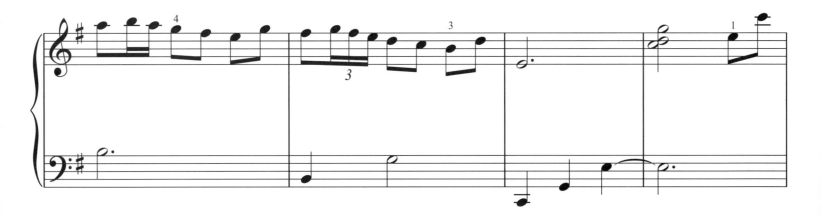

115

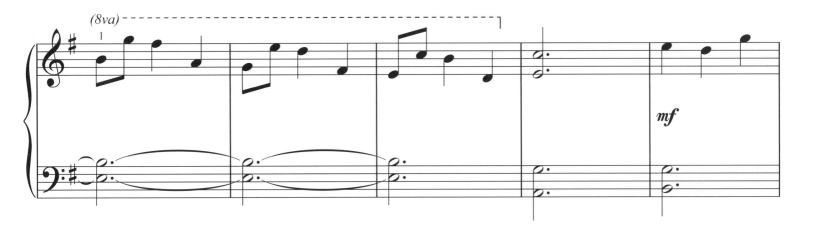

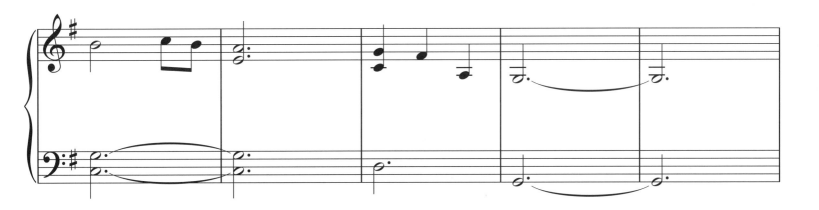

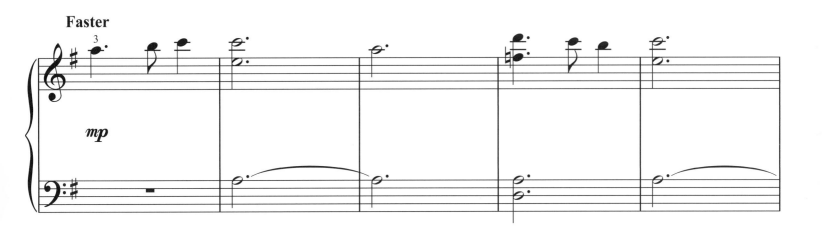

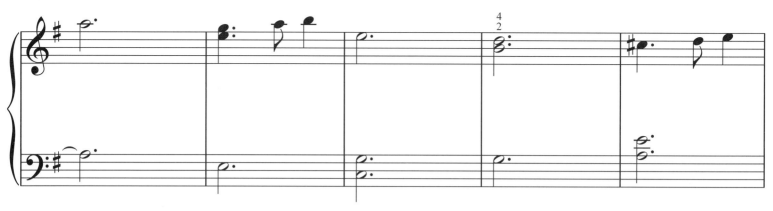

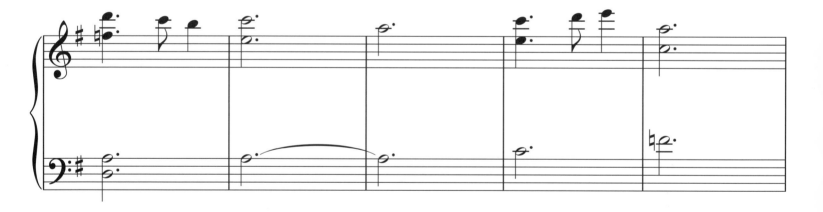

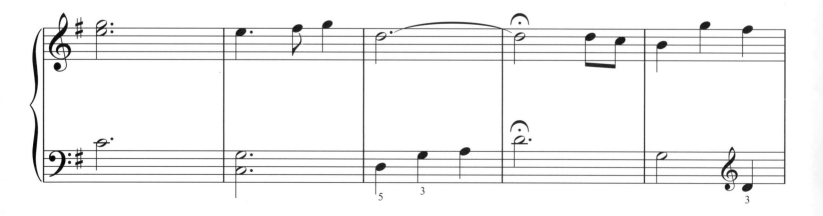

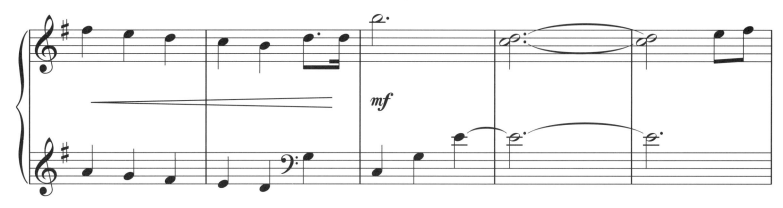

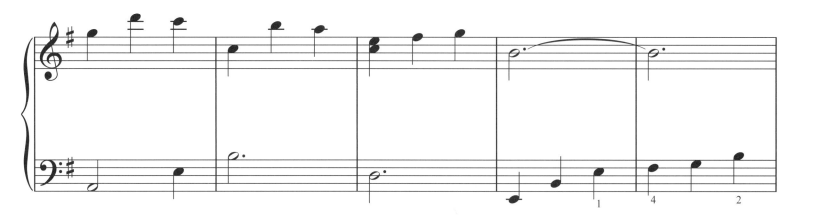

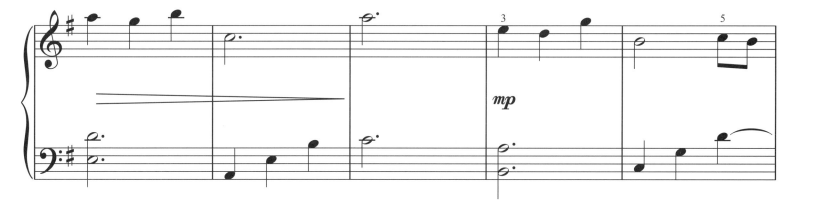

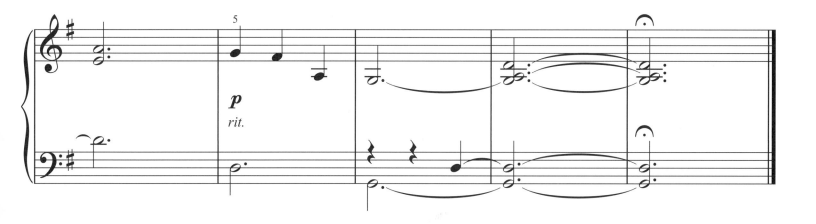

PERHAPS LOVE

Words and Music by
JOHN DENVER

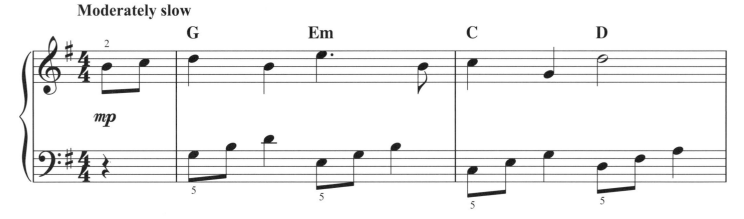

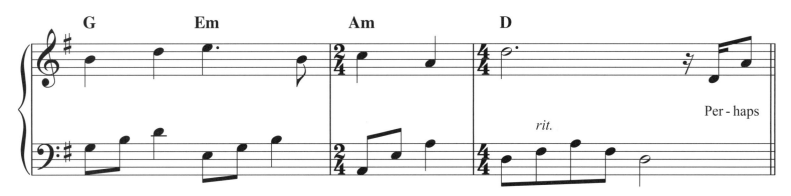

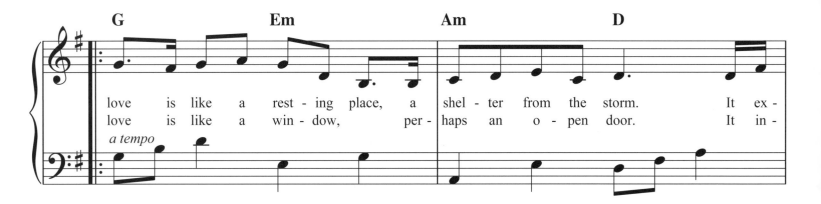

love is like a rest-ing place, a shel-ter from the storm. It ex-
love is like a win-dow, per-haps an o-pen door. It in-

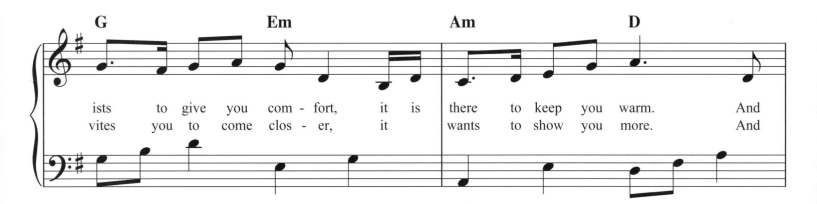

ists to give you com-fort, it is there to keep you warm. And
vites you to come clos-er, it wants to show you more. And

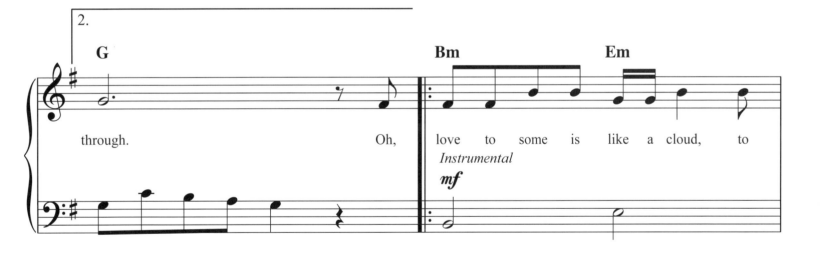

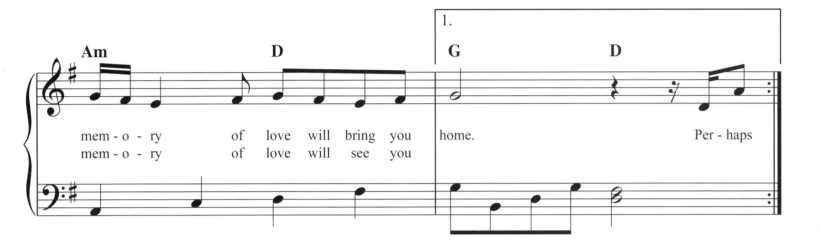

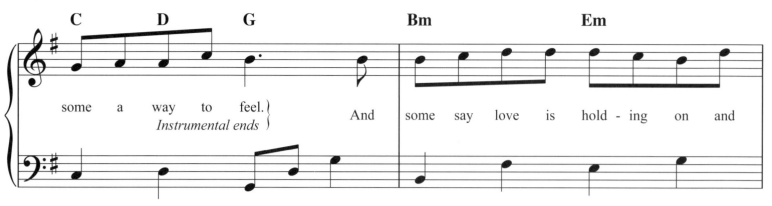

some a way to feel. *Instrumental ends* And some say love is hold-ing on and

some say let-ting go. And some say love is ev-'ry-thing,

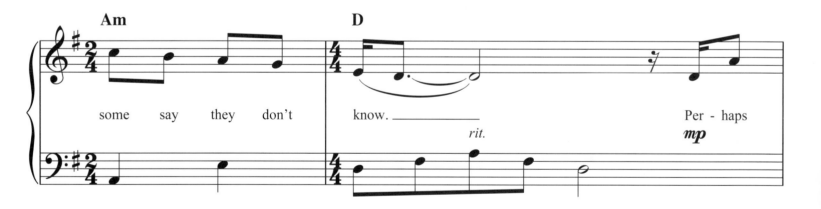

some say they don't know. _____ *rit.* Per-haps **mp**

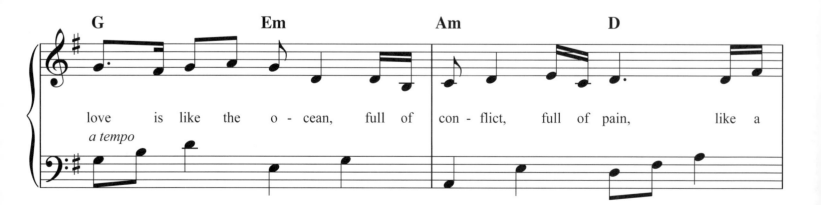

a tempo love is like the o-cean, full of con-flict, full of pain, like a

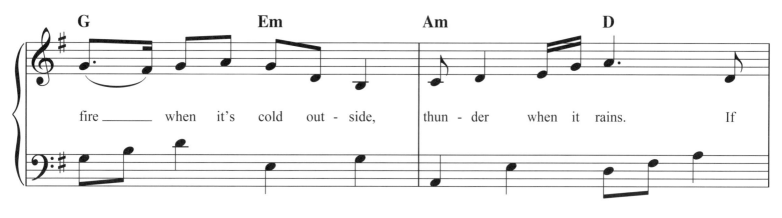

fire _____ when it's cold out - side, thun - der when it rains. If

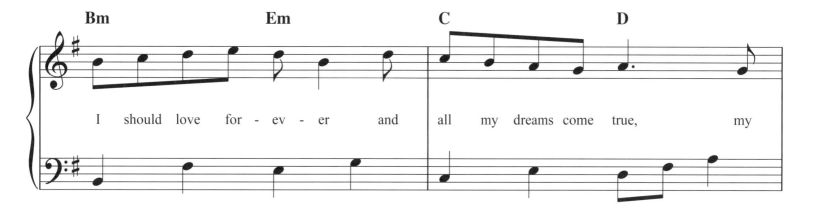

I should love for - ev - er and all my dreams come true, my

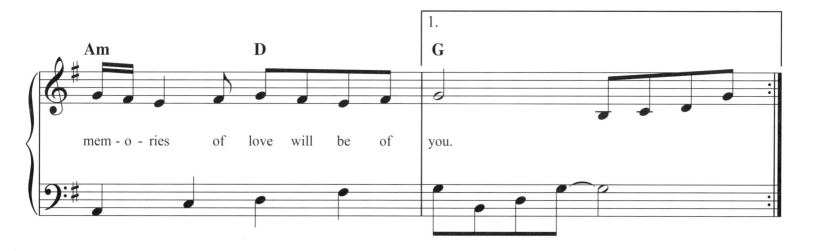

1.

mem - o - ries of love will be of you.

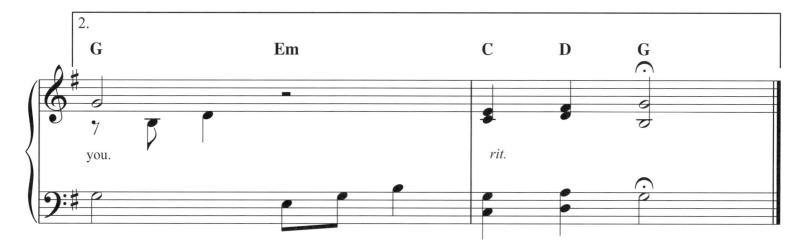

2.

you.

rit.

SOMEWHERE IN TIME
from SOMEWHERE IN TIME

By JOHN BARRY

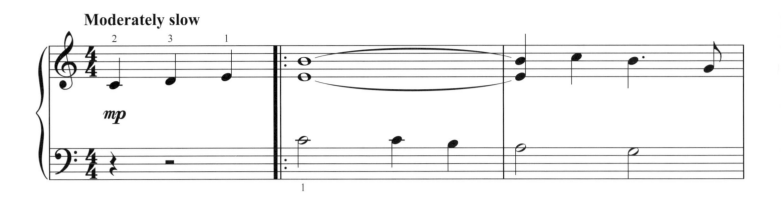

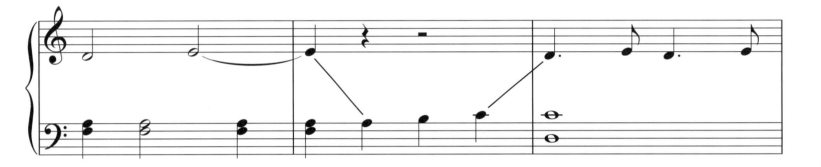

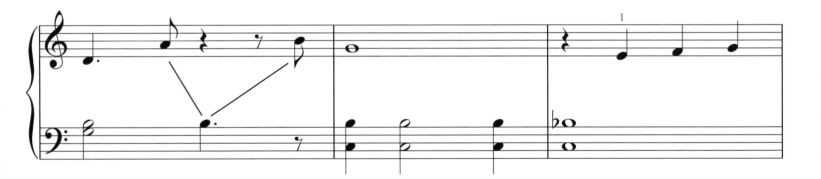

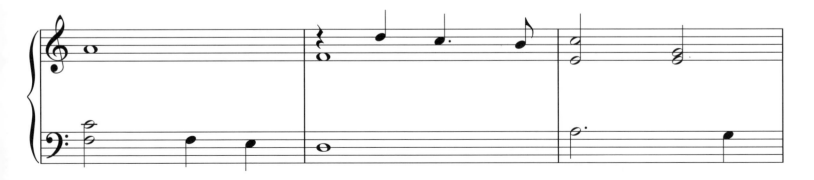

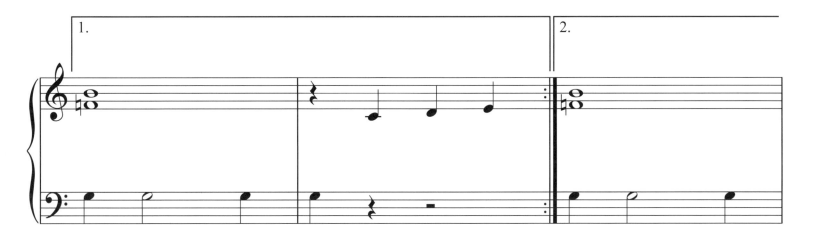

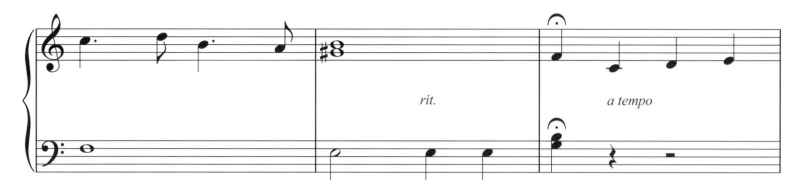

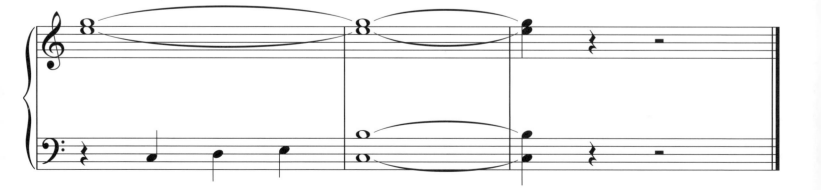

THE ROSE
from the Twentieth Century-Fox Motion Picture Release THE ROSE

Words and Music by
AMANDA McBROOM

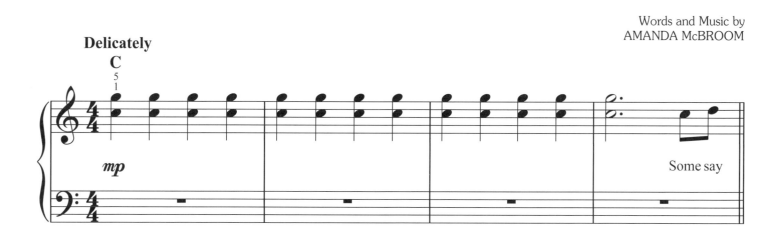

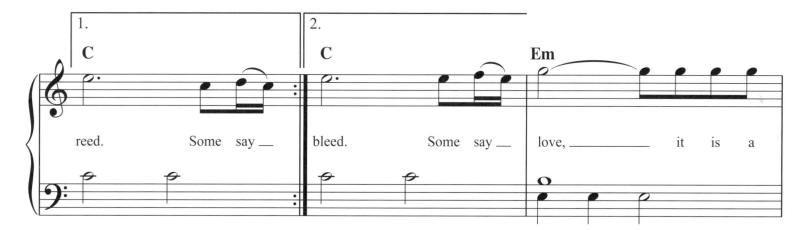

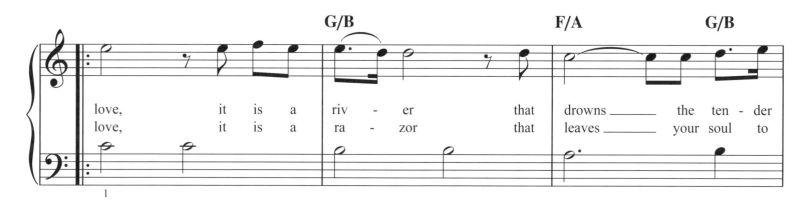

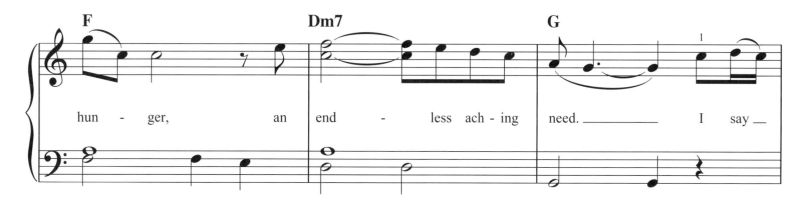

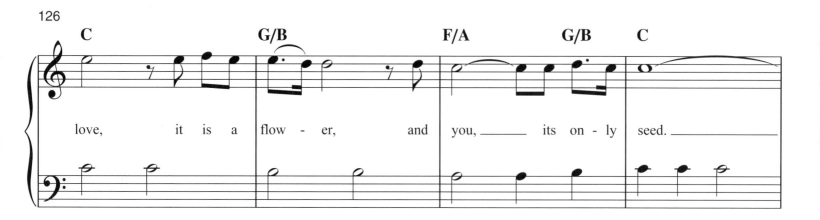

love, it is a flow - er, and you, _____ its on - ly seed. _____

_____ It's the _ heart a - fraid of break - ing that
night has been too lone - ly and the

nev - er _____ learns to _ dance. It's the _ dream _____ a - fraid of wak - ing that
road _____ has been too _ long, and you think _____ that love is on - ly for the

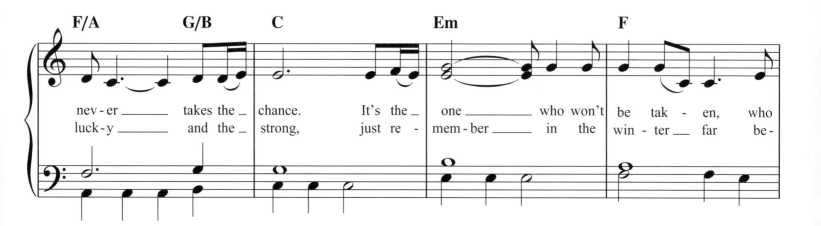

nev - er _____ takes the _ chance. It's the _ one _____ who won't be tak - en, who
luck - y _____ and the _ strong, just re - mem - ber _____ in the win - ter _ far be -

can - not seem to give, _____ and the __ soul a - fraid of
neath _____ the bit - ter snows _____ lies the __ seed that with the

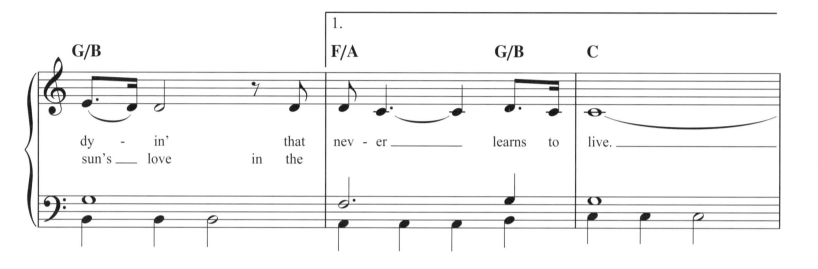

1.

dy - in' that nev - er _____ learns to live. _____
sun's __ love in the

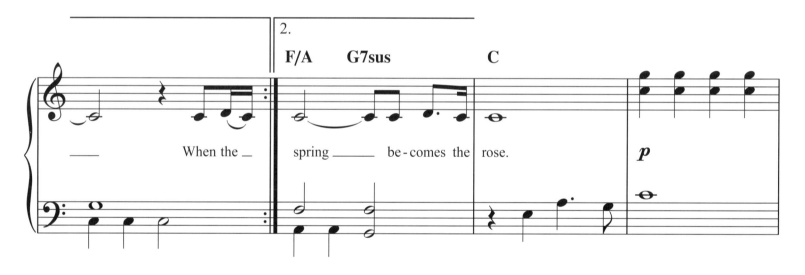

2.

___ When the __ spring _____ be - comes the rose.

p

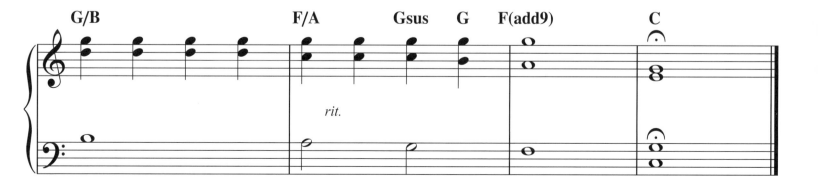

rit.

SOMEONE LIKE YOU

Words and Music by ADELE ADKINS
and DAN WILSON

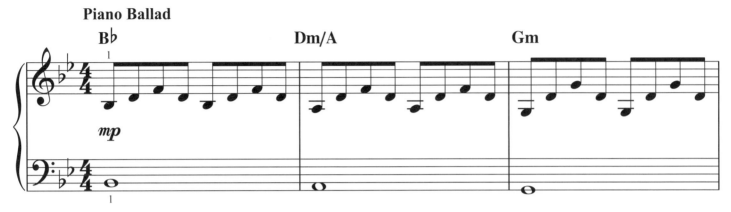

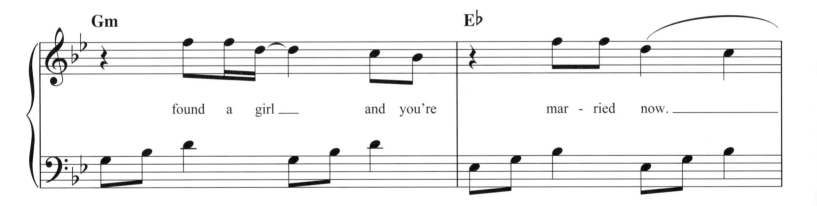

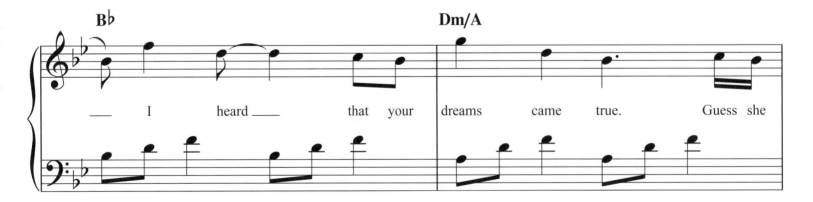

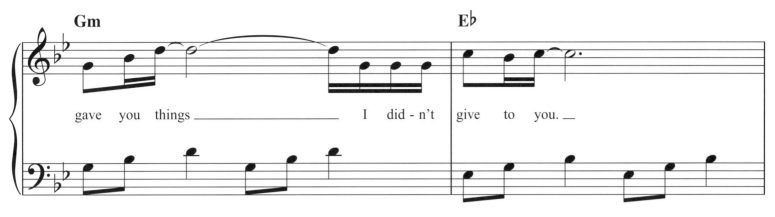

gave you things _____ I did-n't give to you. __

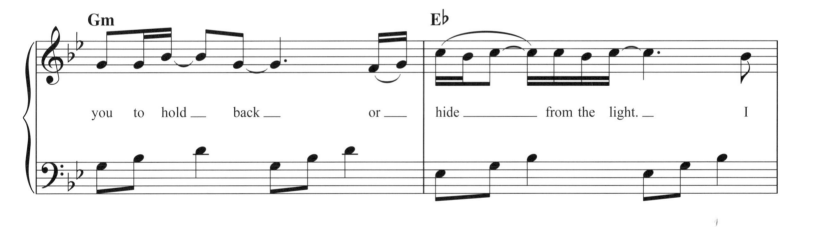

Old friend, why are you so ___ shy? Ain't like

you to hold __ back __ or __ hide _____ from the light. __ I

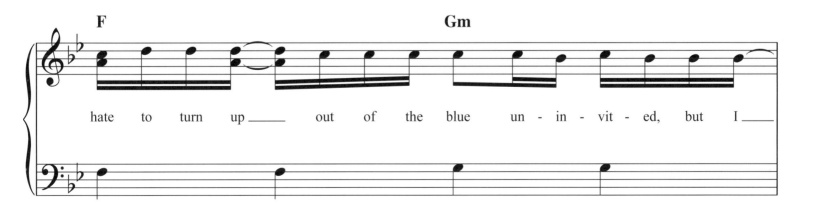

hate to turn up ___ out of the blue un-in-vit-ed, but I ___

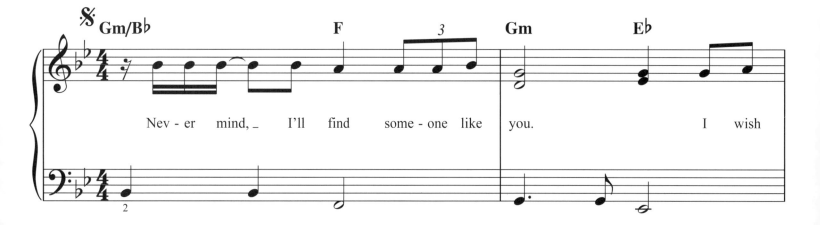

noth - ing but ___ the best for you, too. Don't for -

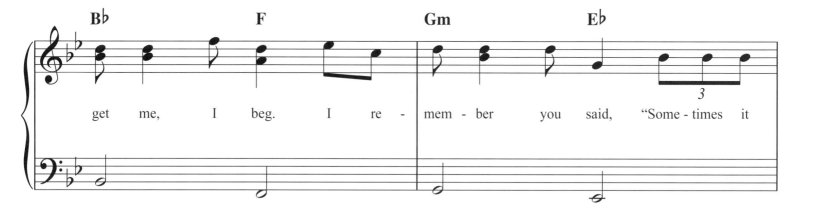

get me, I beg. I re - mem - ber you said, "Some - times it

To Coda ⊕

lasts in love, but some - times it hurts in - stead." Some - times it

lasts in love, but some - times it hurts in - stead. ___

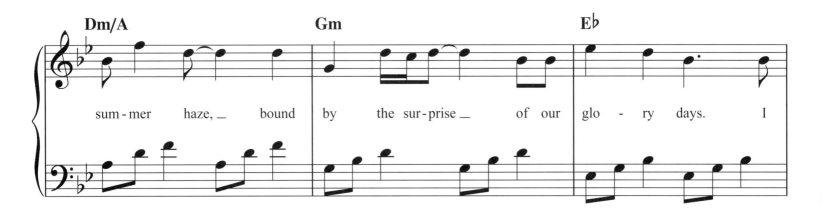

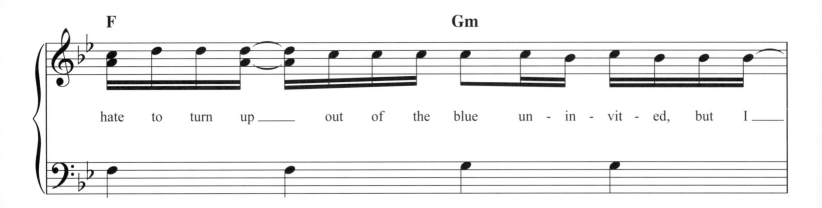

_____ could - n't stay a - way, _____ I could - n't fight it. I had

hoped you'd see my face and that you'd be re - mind - ed that, for

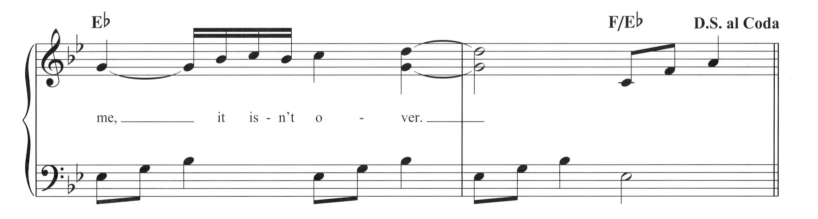

me, _____ it is - n't o - ver. _____

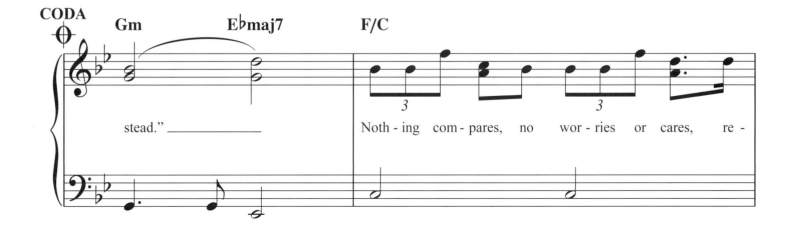

stead." _____   Noth - ing com - pares, no wor - ries or cares, re -

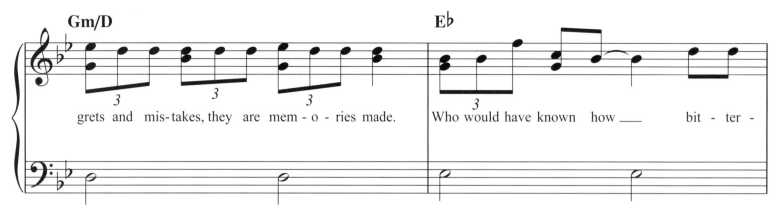

grets and mis-takes, they are mem - o - ries made. Who would have known how ____ bit - ter -

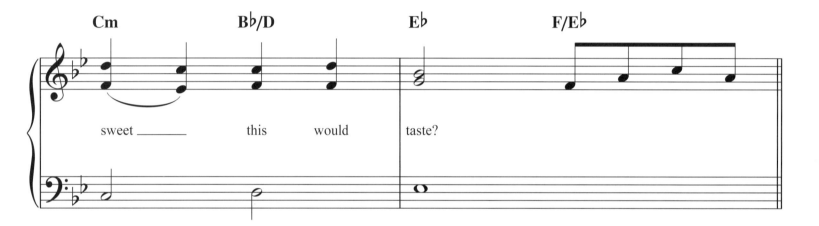

sweet _____ this would taste?

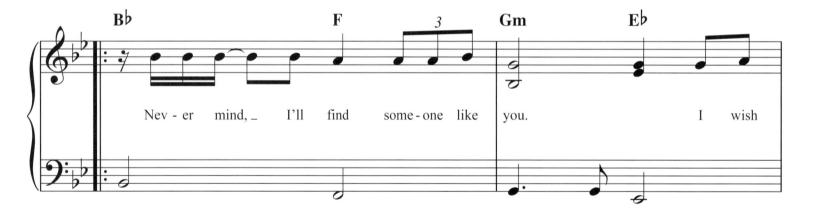

Nev - er mind, __ I'll find some - one like you. I wish

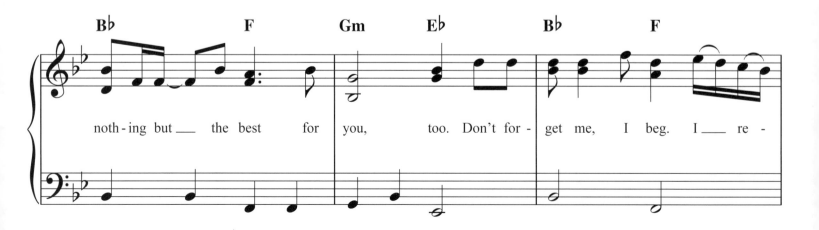

noth - ing but __ the best for you, too. Don't for - get me, I beg. I __ re -

mem - ber you said, "Some - times it lasts in love, but some - times it hurts in -

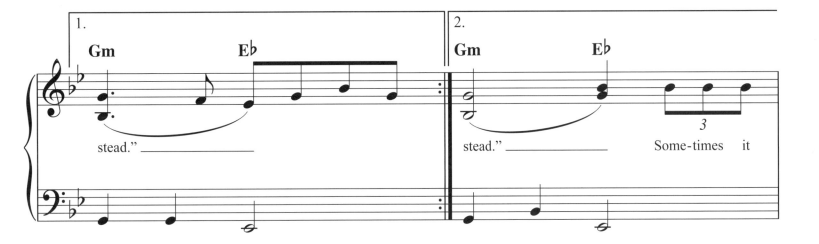

1. stead." _____ 2. stead." _____ Some - times it

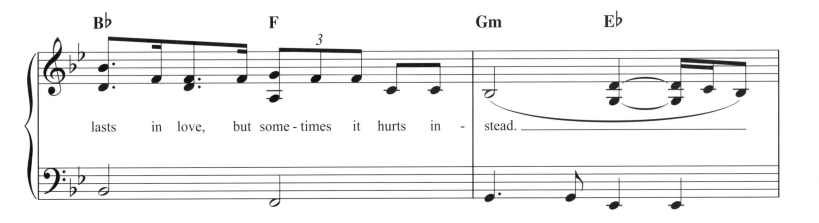

lasts in love, but some - times it hurts in - stead. _____

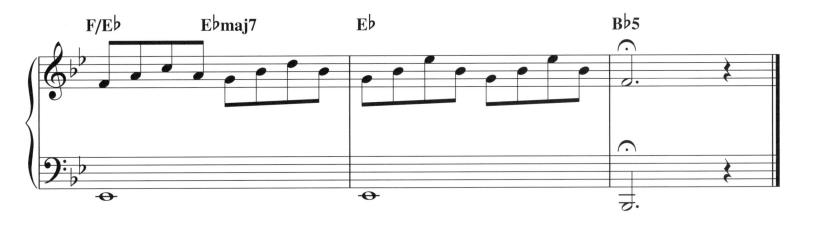

(Theme from)
A SUMMER PLACE
from A SUMMER PLACE

Words by MACK DISCANT
Music by MAX STEINER

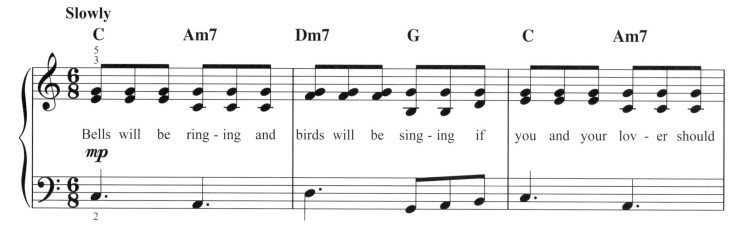

Bells will be ring-ing and birds will be sing-ing if you and your lov-er should

ev - er dis - cov - er that there's / There's a sum - mer

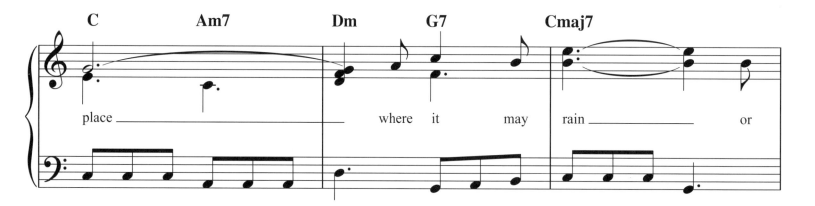

place where it may rain or

storm. Yet I'm safe and warm, for with -

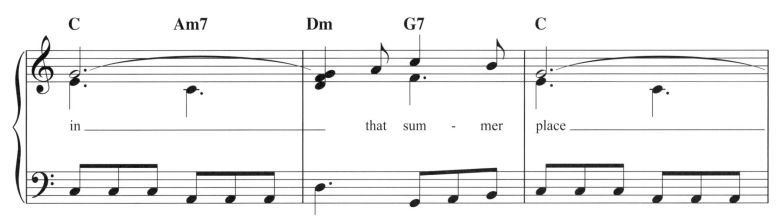

in _____ that sum - mer place _____

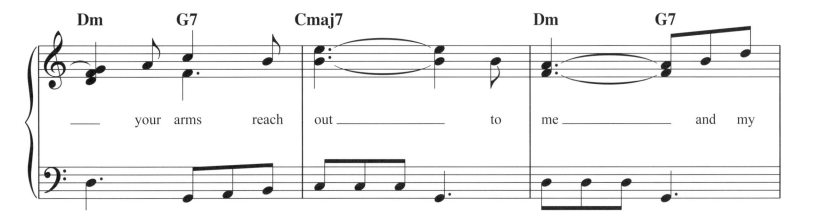

____ your arms reach out _____ to me _____ and my

heart _____ is free _____ from all care. _____

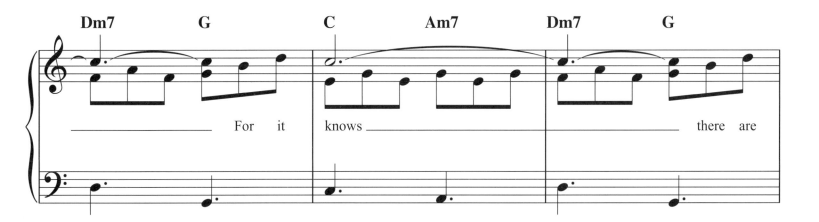

_____ For it knows _____ there are

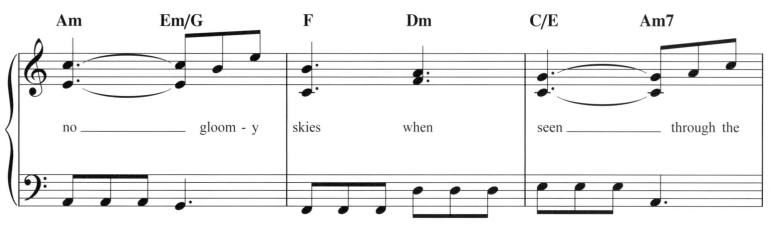

no _____ gloom - y   skies   when   seen _____ through the

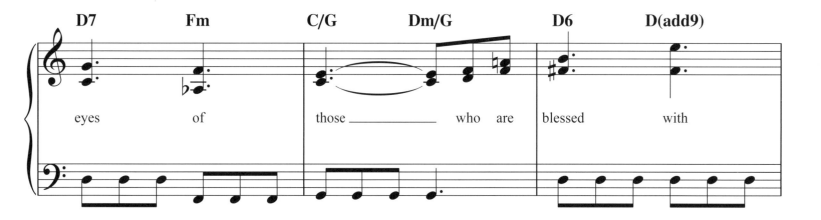

eyes   of   those _____ who   are   blessed   with

love. _____   And   the   sweet   se - cret   of _____

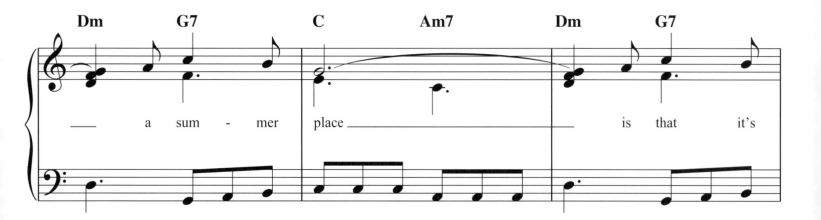

___   a   sum - mer   place _____   is   that   it's

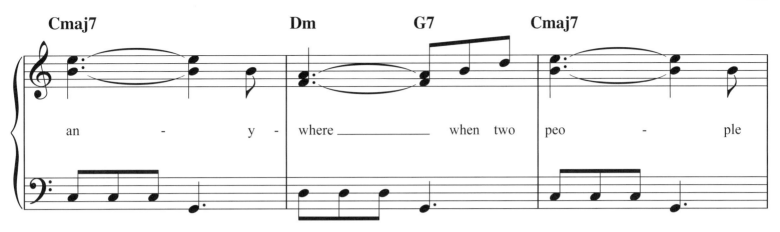

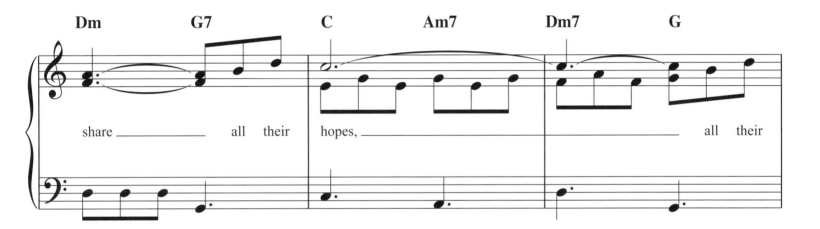

TARA'S THEME
(My Own True Love)
from GONE WITH THE WIND

By MAX STEINER

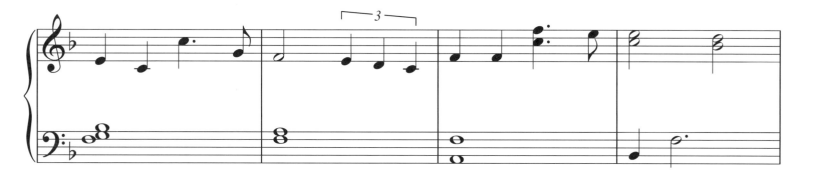

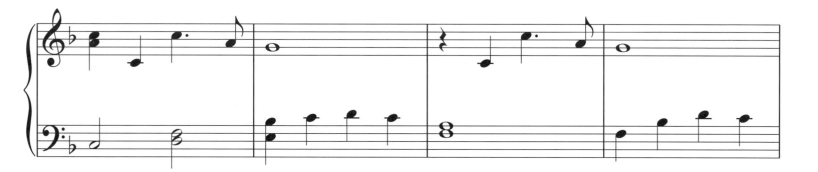

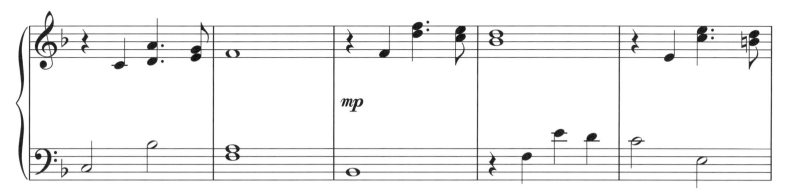

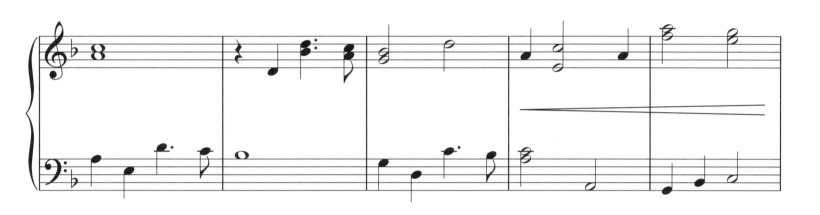

TEARS IN HEAVEN

Words and Music by ERIC CLAPTON
and WILL JENNINGS

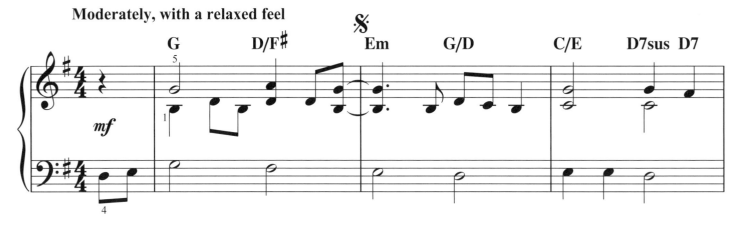

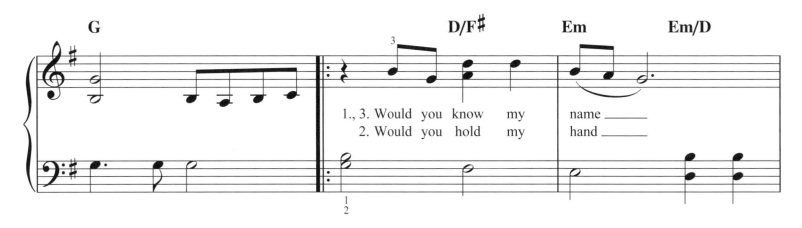

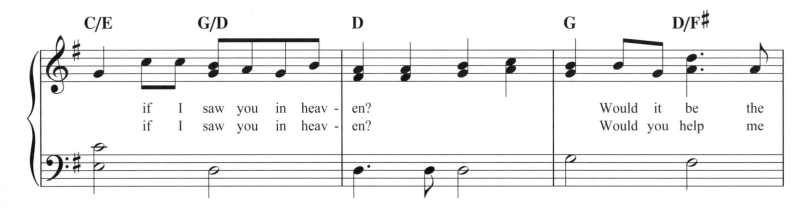

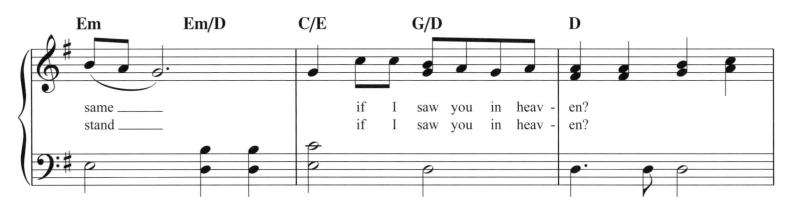

I must be strong _____ and car - ry on _____
I'll find my way _____ through night and day _

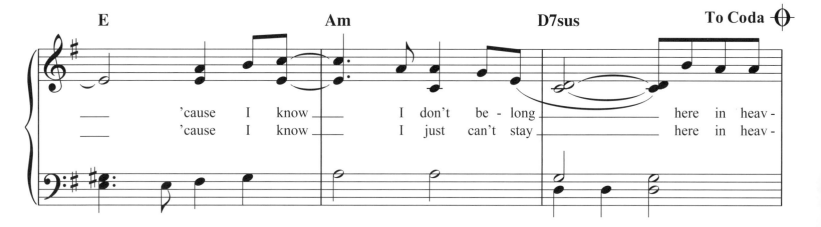

_____ 'cause I know _____ I don't be - long _____ here in heav -
_____ 'cause I know _____ I just can't stay _____ here in heav -

en.
en.

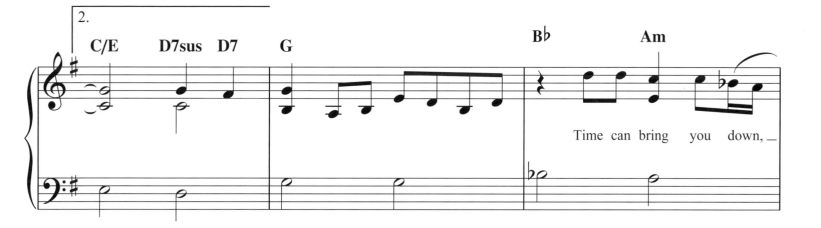

Time can bring you down, _

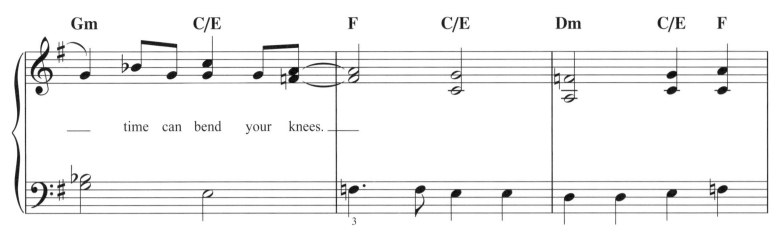

time can bend your knees.

Time can break the heart, _____ have you beg - gin' please, _____ beg - gin' please. _

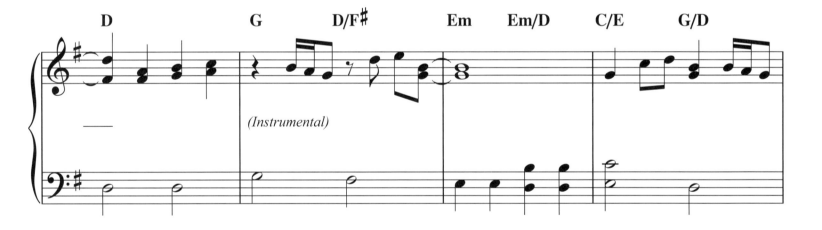

(Instrumental)

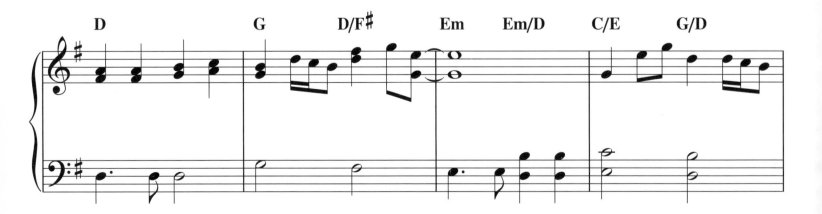

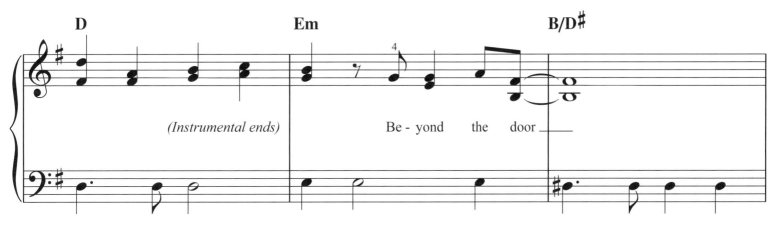

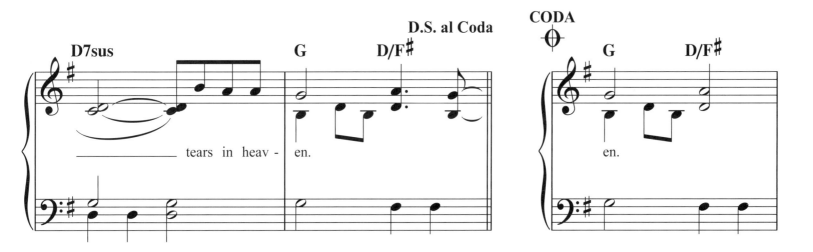

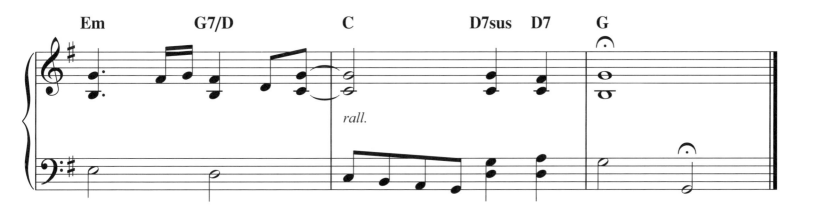

A THOUSAND YEARS

from the Summit Entertainment film THE TWILIGHT SAGA: BREAKING DAWN – PART 1

Words and Music by DAVID HODGES
and CHRISTINA PERRI

Moderately, in one

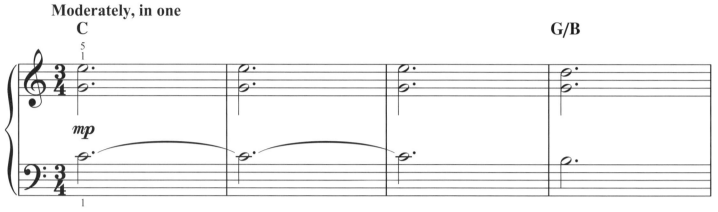

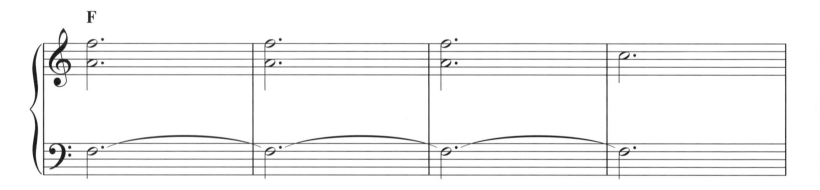

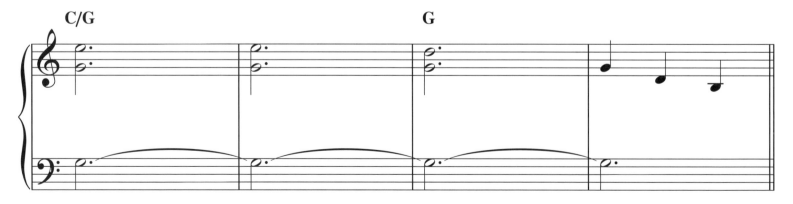

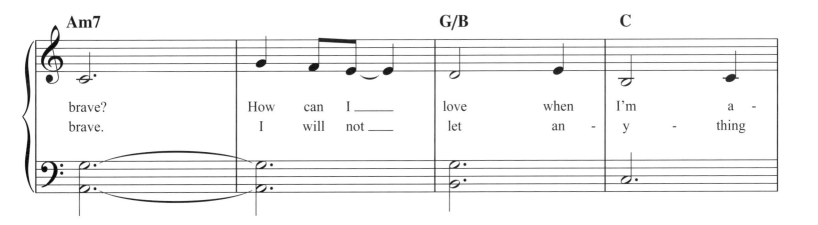

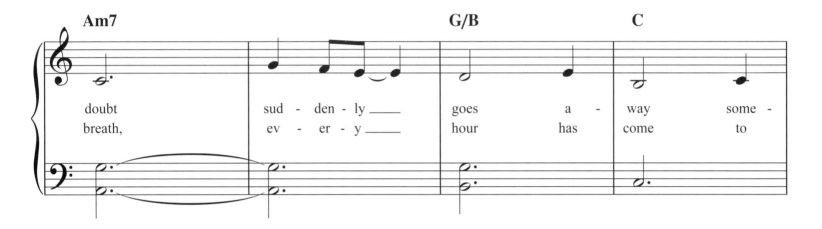

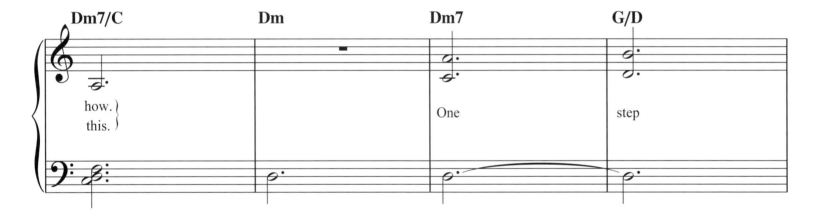

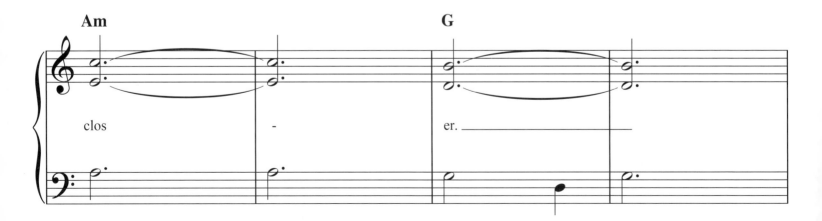

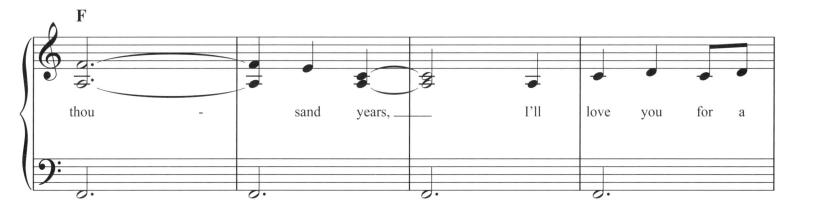

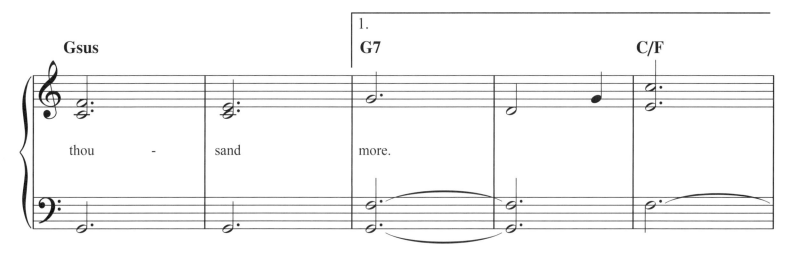

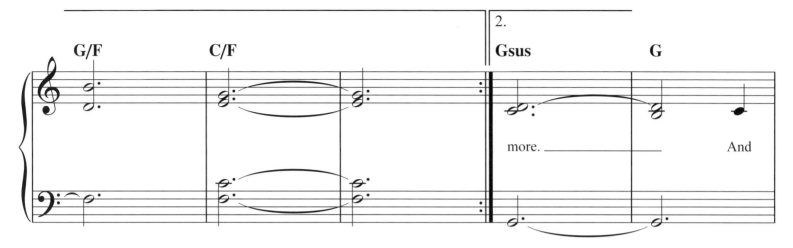

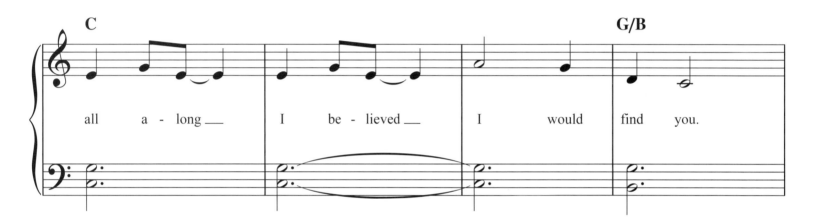

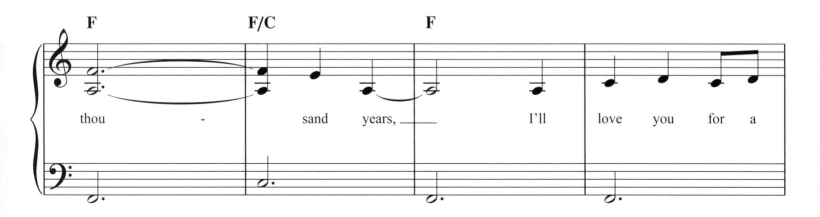

To Coda ⊕

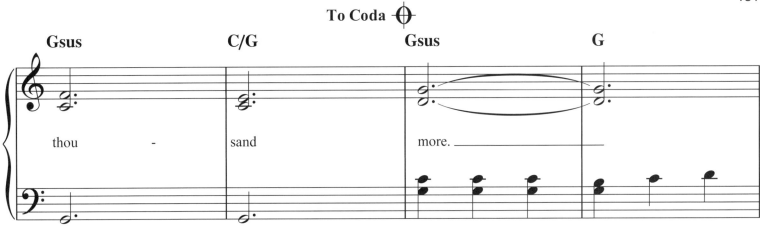

thou - sand   more. _____

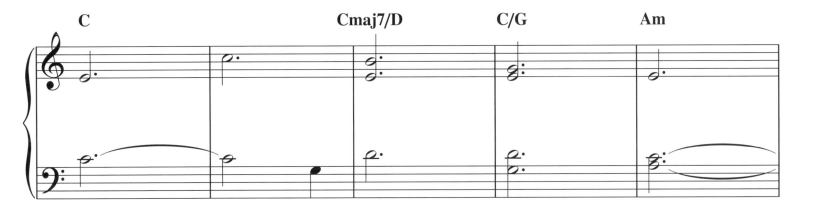

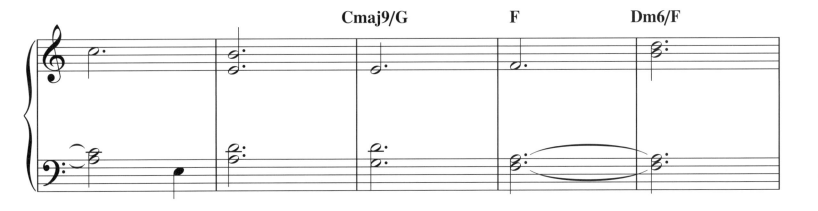

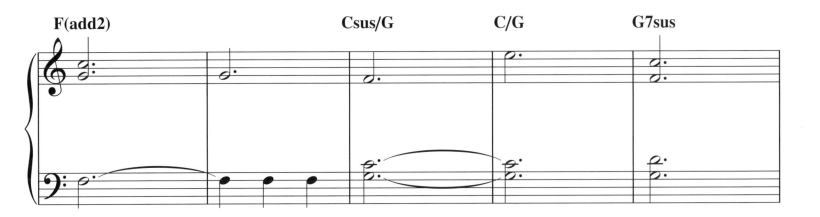

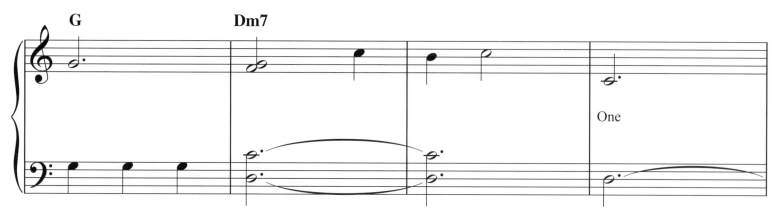

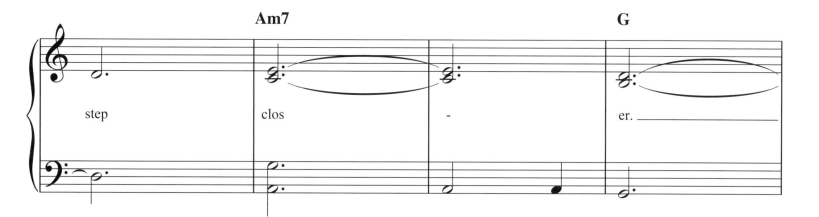

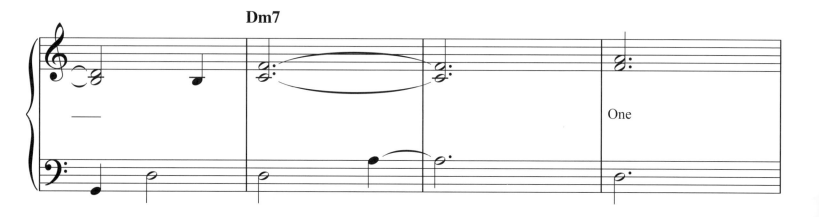

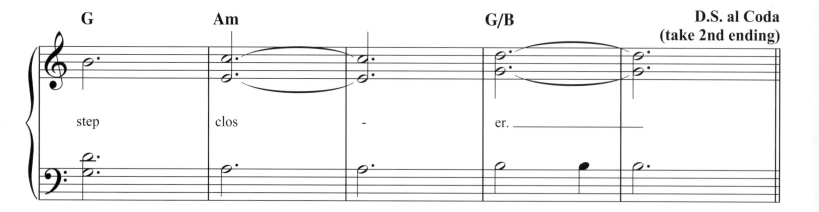

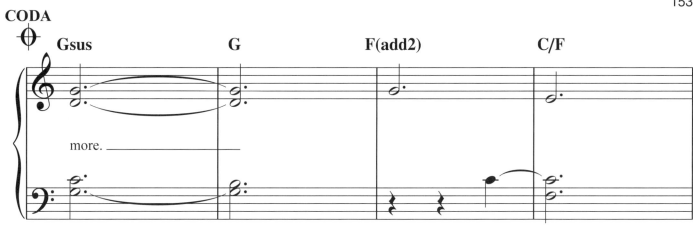

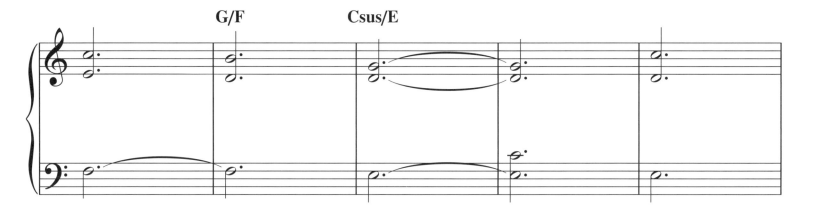

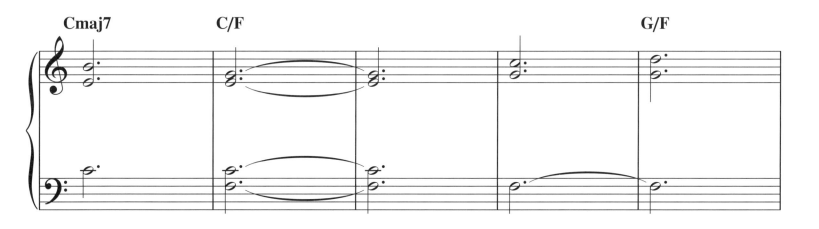

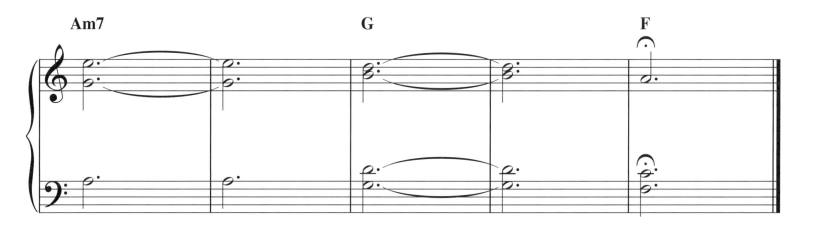

TIME AFTER TIME

from the Metro-Goldwyn-Mayer Picture IT HAPPENED IN BROOKLYN

Words by SAMMY CAHN
Music by JULE STYNE

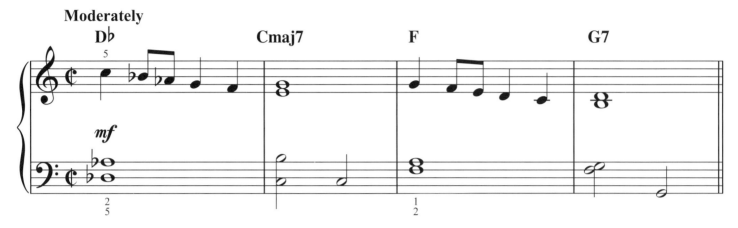

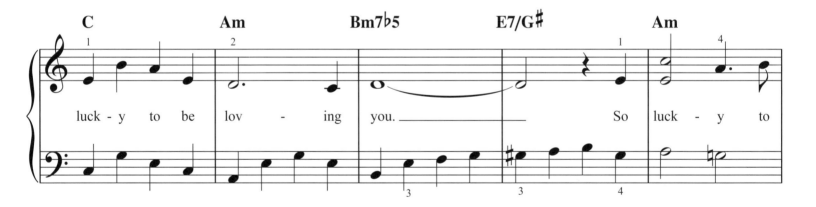

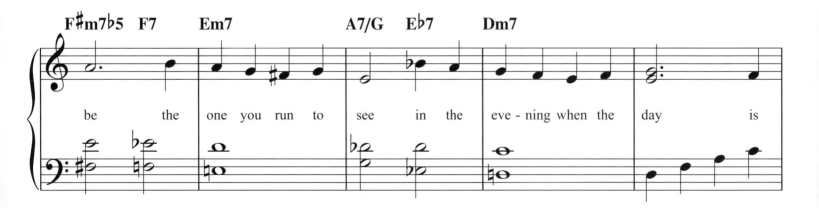

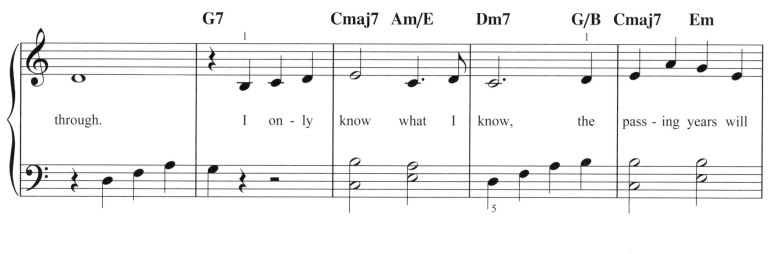

through. I on-ly know what I know, the pass-ing years will

show you've kept my love so young, so new. And

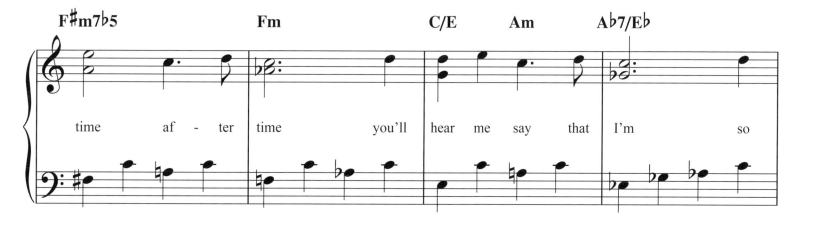

time af-ter time you'll hear me say that I'm so

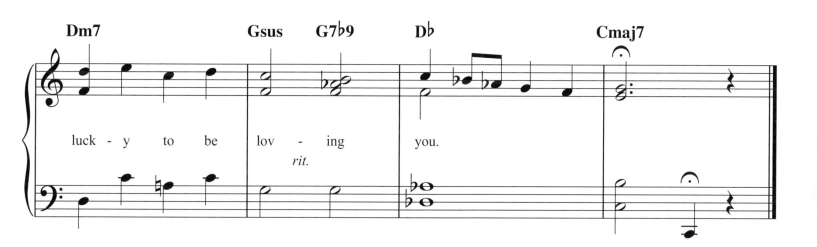

luck-y to be lov-ing you.

rit.

A TIME FOR US
(Love Theme)
from the Paramount Picture ROMEO AND JULIET

Words by LARRY KUSIK and EDDIE SNYDER
Music by NINO ROTA

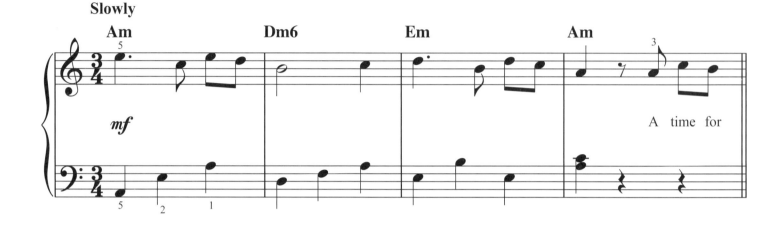

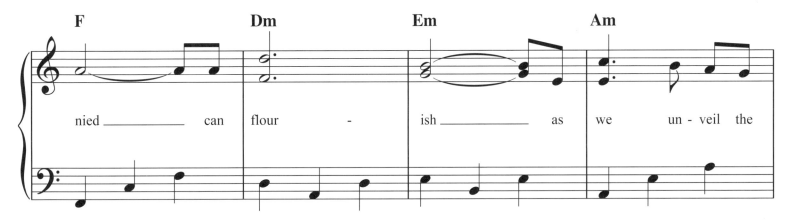

nied _____ can flour - ish _____ as we un - veil the

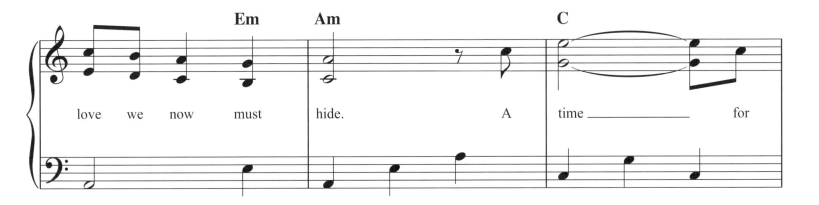

love we now must hide. A time _____ for

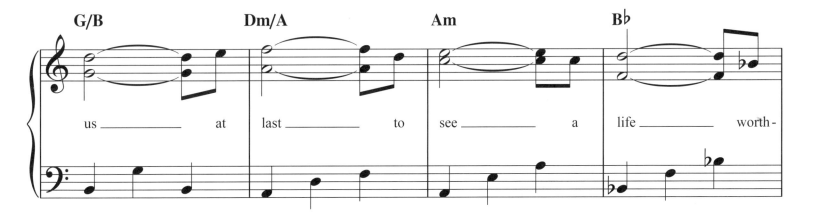

us _____ at last _____ to see _____ a life _____ worth -

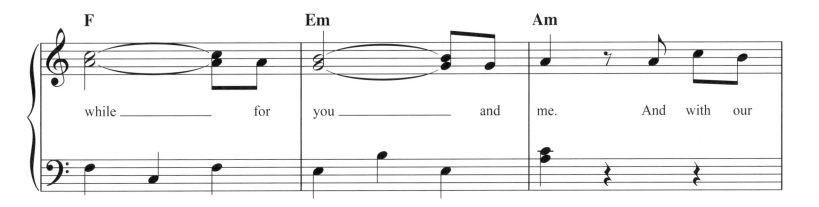

while _____ for you _____ and me. And with our

love, through tears and thorns, we will en - dure as we pass

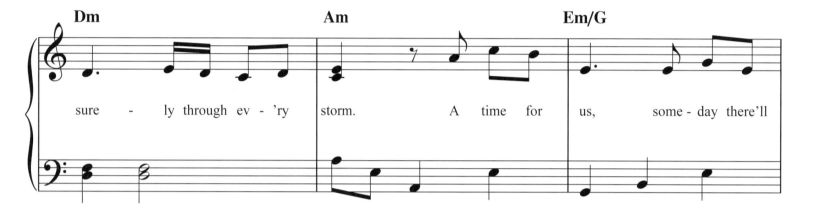

sure - ly through ev - 'ry storm. A time for us, some - day there'll

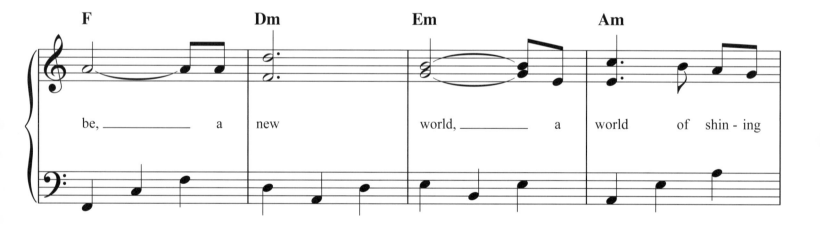

be, _____ a new world, _____ a world of shin - ing

hope for you and me. A time for me.
rit.

UNFORGETTABLE

Words and Music by
IRVING GORDON

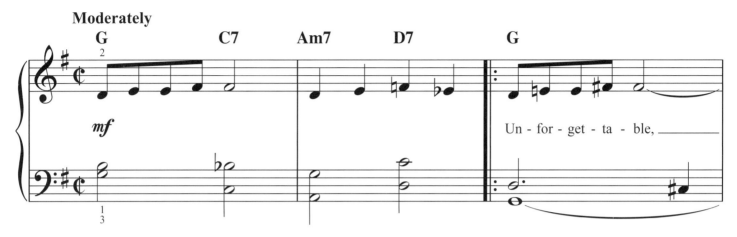

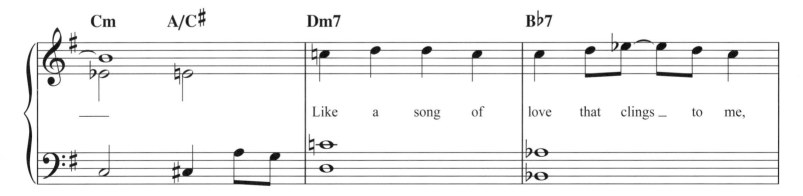

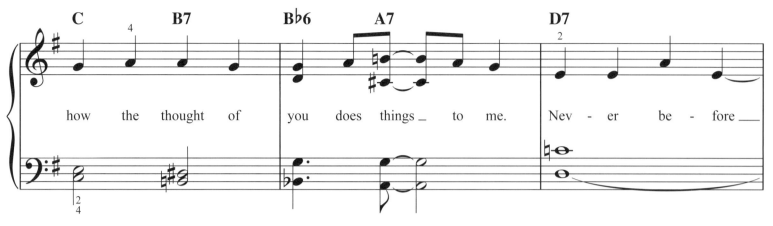

how the thought of you does things _ to me. Nev - er be - fore _

_ has some - one been more _

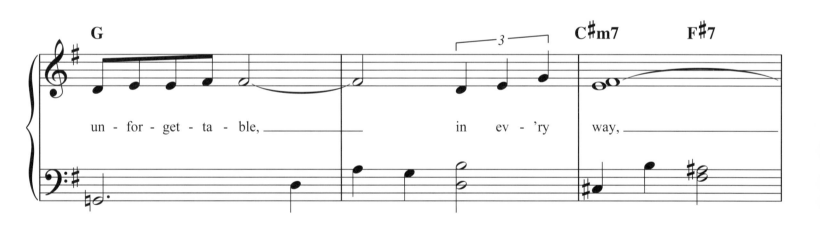

un - for - get - ta - ble, _ in ev - 'ry way, _

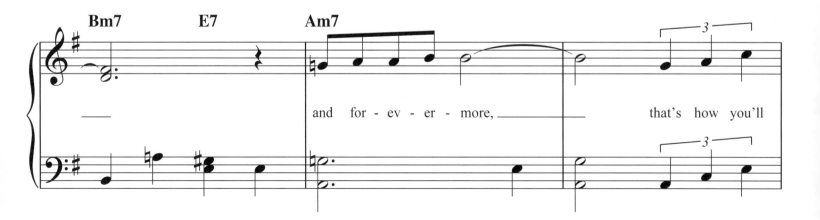

and for - ev - er - more, _ that's how you'll

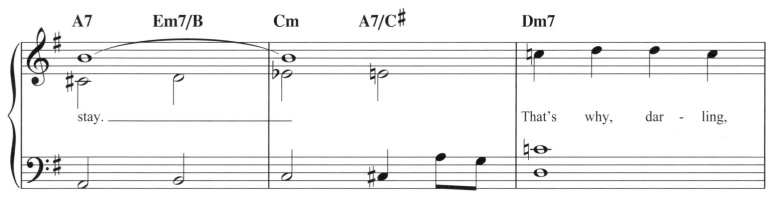

stay. _____ That's why, dar - ling,

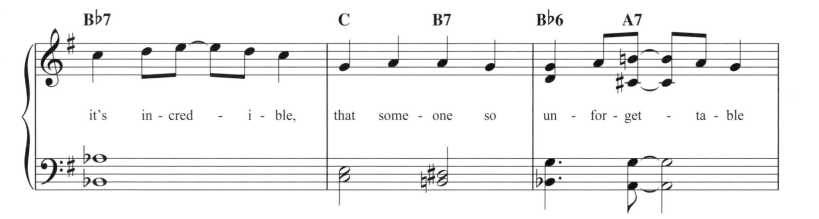

it's in - cred - i - ble, that some - one so un - for - get - ta - ble

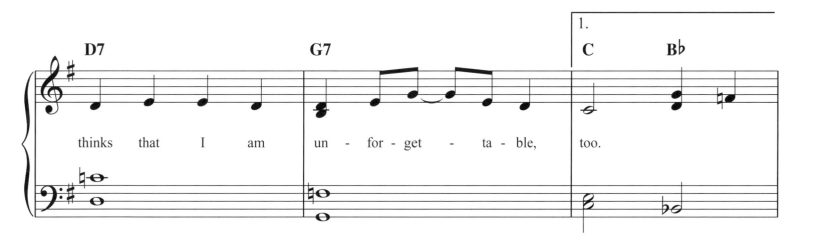

thinks that I am un - for - get - ta - ble, too.

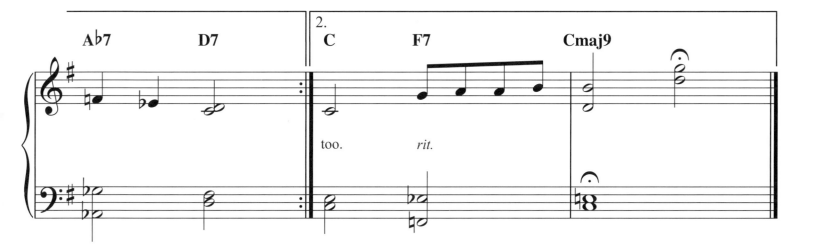

too. *rit.*

WATERMARK

Music by ENYA
Words by ROMA RYAN

Slowly, with freedom

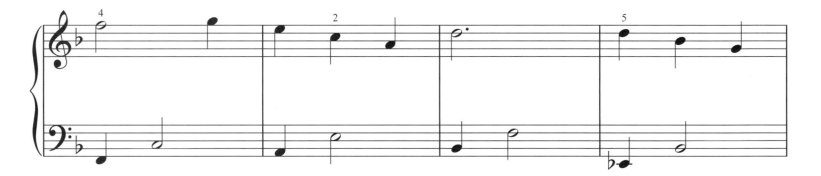

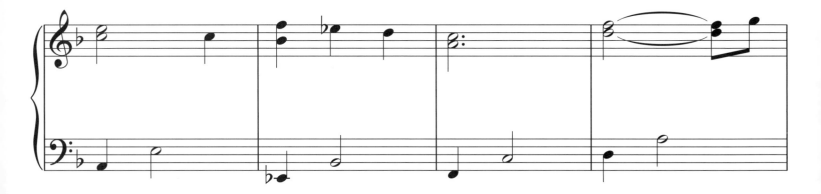

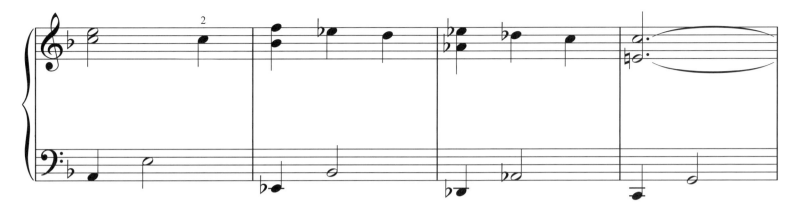

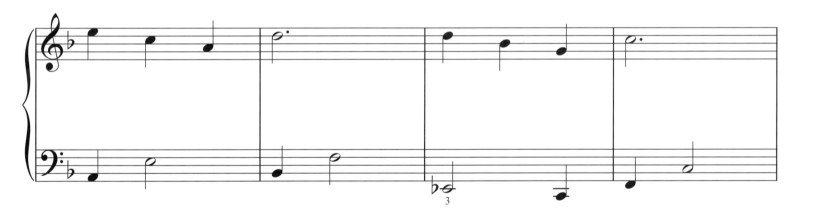

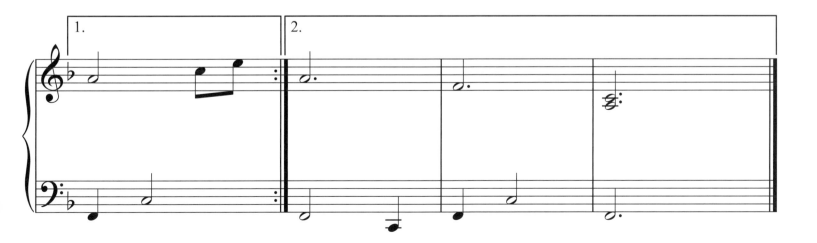

THE WAY WE WERE

from the Motion Picture THE WAY WE WERE

Words by ALAN and MARILYN BERGMAN
Music by MARVIN HAMLISCH

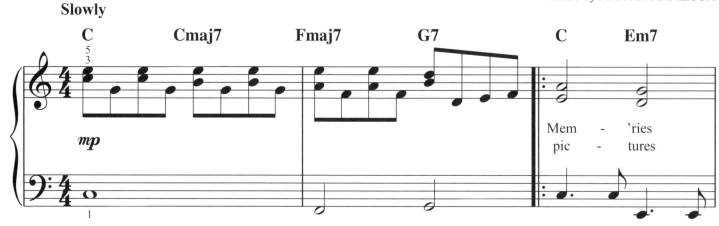

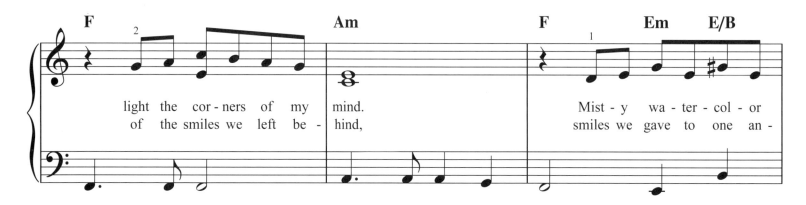

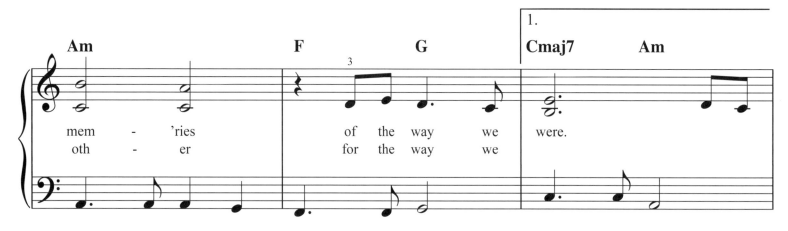

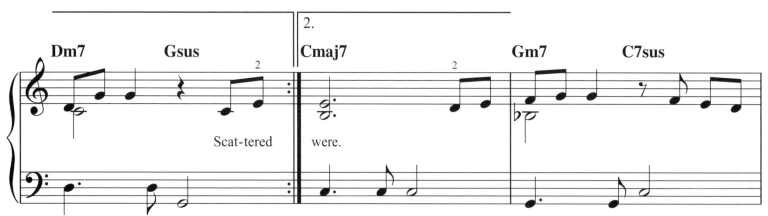

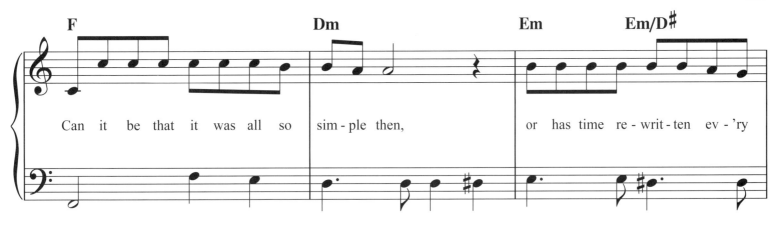

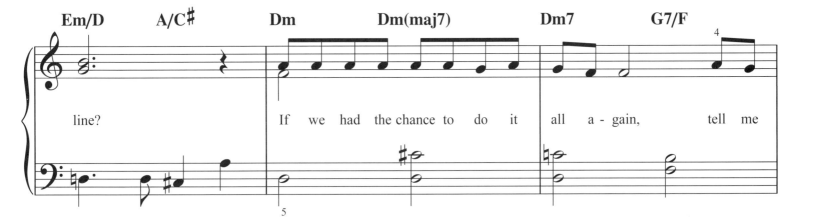

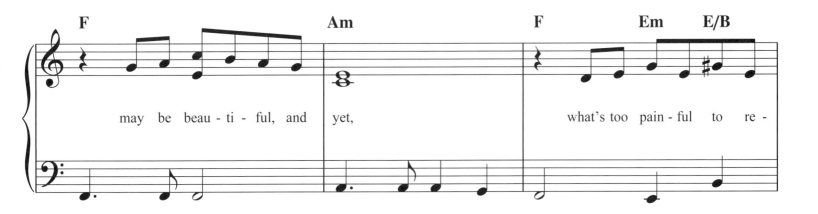

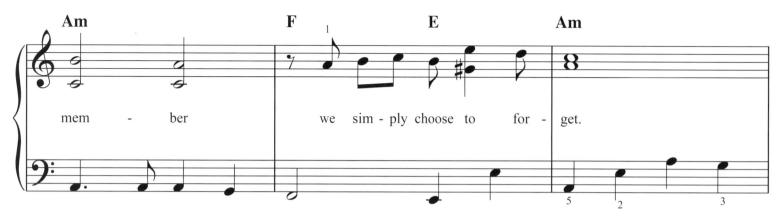

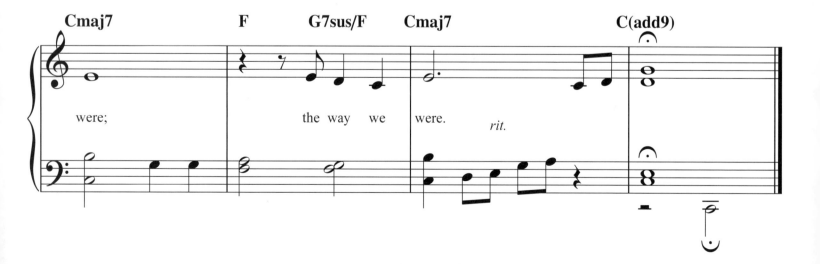

WHITE FLAG

Words and Music by RICK NOWELS,
ROLLO ARMSTRONG and DIDO ARMSTRONG

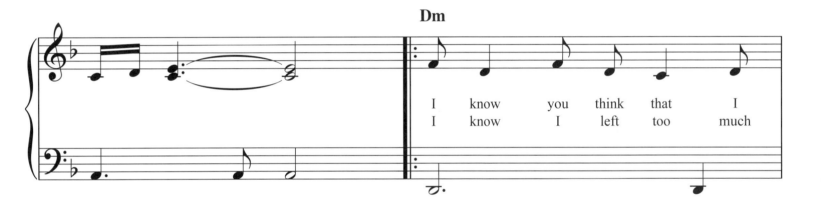

I know you think that I
I know I left too much

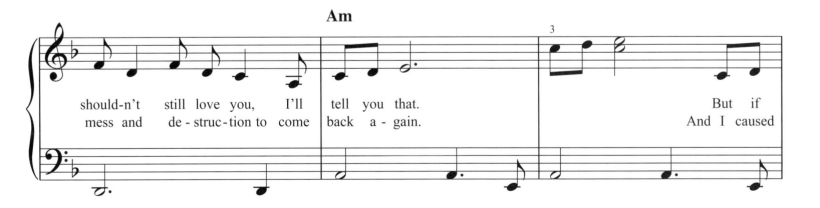

should-n't still love you, I'll tell you that. But if
mess and de-struc-tion to come back a-gain. And I caused

Dm

I did -- n't say it, well, I'd still have felt it. ____
noth -- ing but trou -- ble; I un -- der -- stand if you can't

Am

Where's the sense in that? ____ I prom -- ise
talk to me a -- gain. ____

C

I'm not try -- ing to make ____ your life hard -- er; I'll re --
And if you live by the rules ____ that it's o -- ver, then I'm

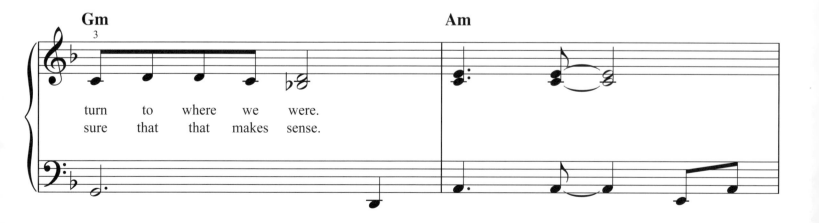

Gm   **Am**

turn to where we were.
sure that that makes sense.

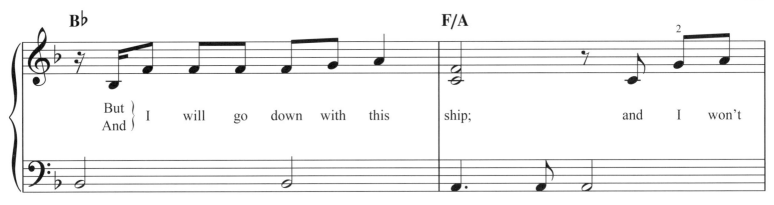

But
And } I will go down with this ship; and I won't

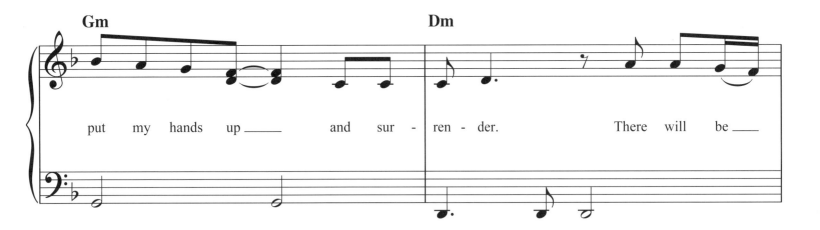

put my hands up ____ and sur - ren - der. There will be ____

no white flag a - bove my door; I'm in love and al - ways ____

1.
love and al - ways ____

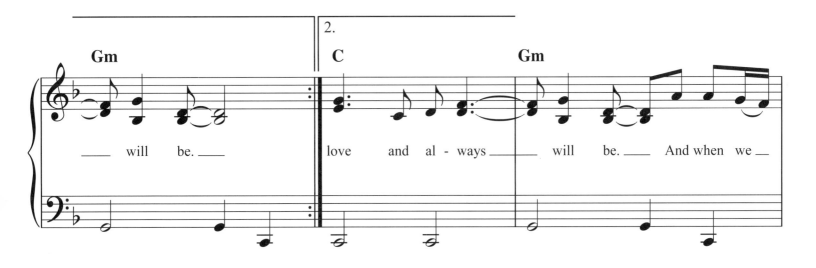

____ will be. ____ love and al - ways ____ will be. ____ And when we ____

meet,   which I'm sure we   will,   all that was _ there _   will be there _

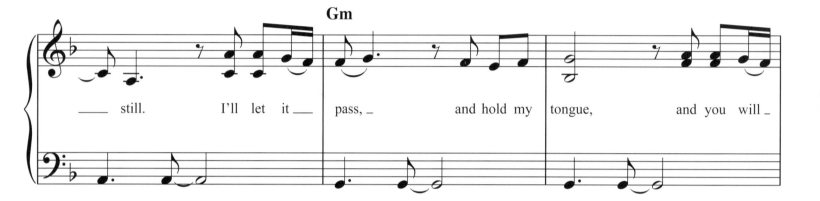

_ still.   I'll let it __ pass, _   and hold my   tongue,   and you will _

think _   that I've moved _ on. _____   I will go down with this

ship;   and   I won't   put   my hands up ___ and sur - ren - der.   There will be _

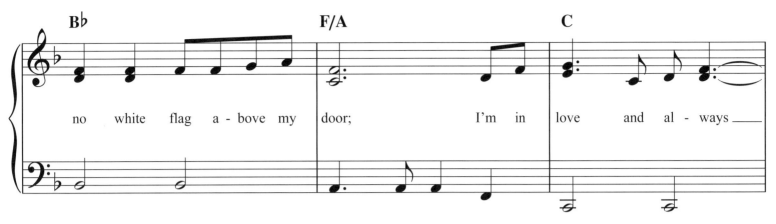

B♭ **F/A** **C**

no white flag a - bove my door; I'm in love and al - ways ___

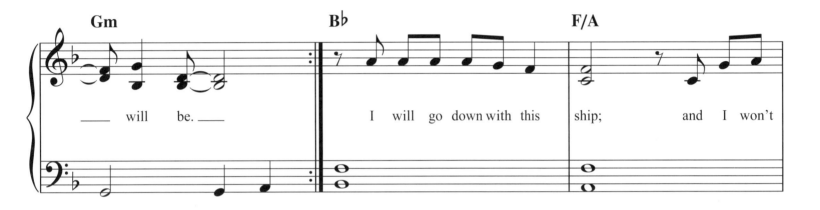

Gm **B♭** **F/A**

___ will be. ___ I will go down with this ship; and I won't

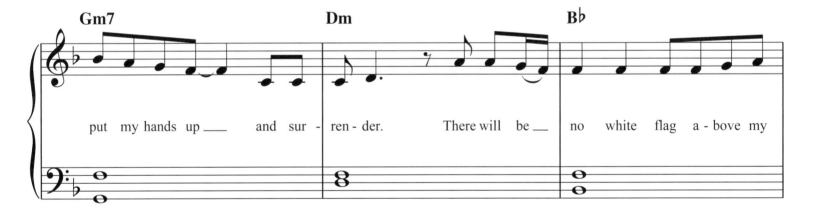

Gm7 **Dm** **B♭**

put my hands up ___ and sur - ren - der. There will be ___ no white flag a - bove my

F/A **C** **Gm**

door; I'm in love and al - ways ___ ___ will be. ___

WHERE DO I BEGIN

(Love Theme)

from the Paramount Picture LOVE STORY

Words by CARL SIGMAN
Music by FRANCIS LAI

Where do I be - gin _____ to tell the sto - ry of how
With her first hel - lo _____ she gave a mean - ing to this

great a love can be, _____ the sweet love sto - ry that is
emp - ty world of mine; _____ there'd nev - er be an - oth - er

old - er than the sea, _____ the sim - ple truth a - bout the
love, an - oth - er time. _____ She came in - to my life and

E | **E7** 1. | **Am**

love she brings to me? Where do I start?
made the liv - ing fine.

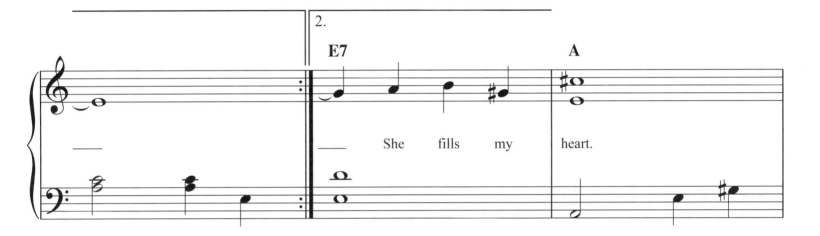

2. **E7** | **A**

She fills my heart.

A7 | **Dm7** | **G7**

She fills my heart with ver - y spe - cial things, with an - gel

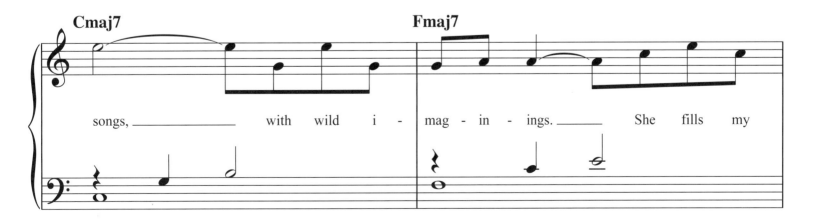

Cmaj7 | **Fmaj7**

songs, with wild i - mag - in - ings. She fills my

soul _____ with so much love that an - y - where I

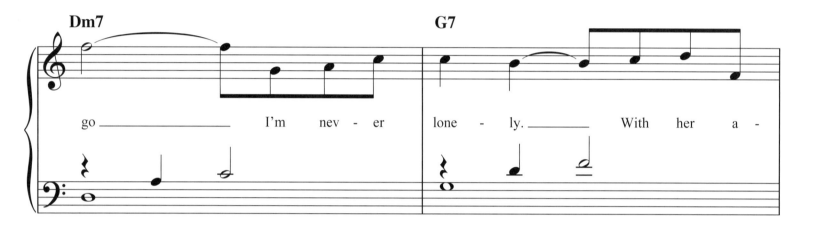

go _____ I'm nev - er lone - ly. _____ With her a -

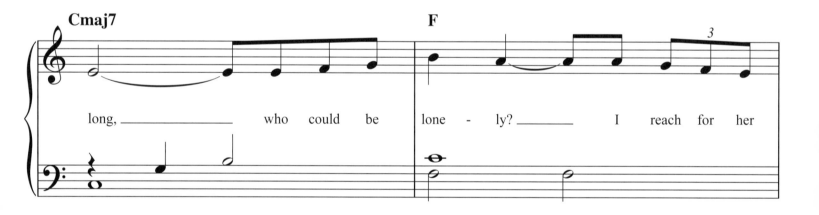

long, _____ who could be lone - ly? _____ I reach for her

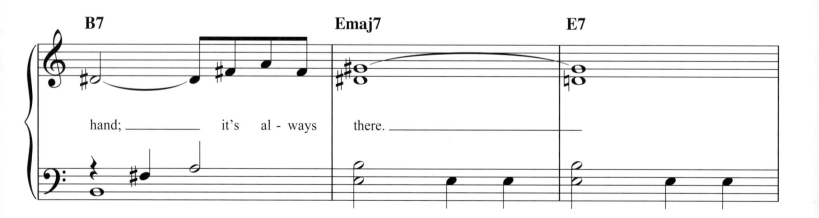

hand; _____ it's al - ways there. _____

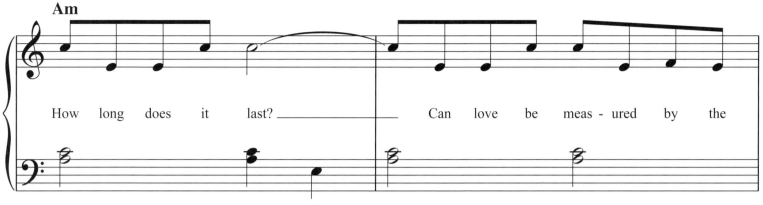

How long does it last? _____ Can love be meas - ured by the

hours in a day? _____ I have no an - swers now, but

this much I can say: _____ I know I'll need her till the stars all burn a - way,

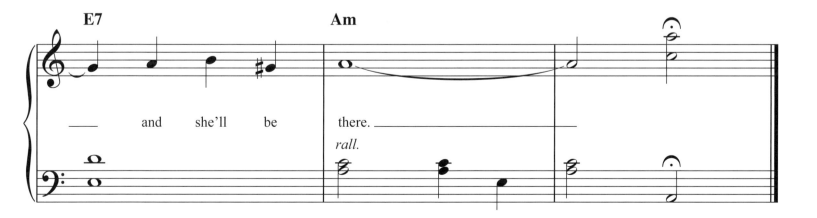

_____ and she'll be there. _____
rall.

THE WIND BENEATH MY WINGS

from the Original Motion Picture BEACHES

Words and Music by LARRY HENLEY
and JEFF SILBAR

Slowly flowing, in 2

It must have been cold ____ there in my
I was the one ____ with all the
It might have ap - peared ____ to go un -

shad - ow, ____
glo - ry, ____
no - ticed ____

to nev - er have sun -
while you were the one ____
that I've got it all ____

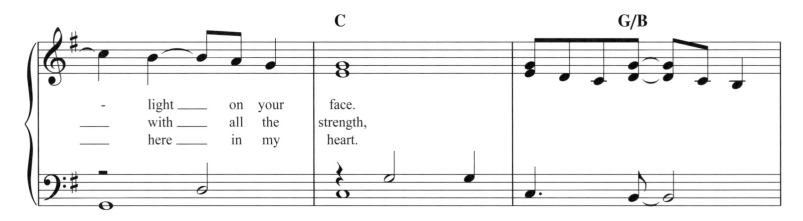

- light ____ on your face.
with ____ all the strength,
here ____ in my heart.

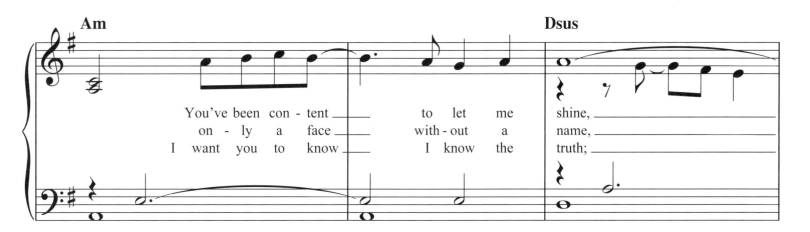

You've been con - tent _____ to let me shine, _____
on - ly a face _____ with - out a name, _____
I want you to know _____ I know the truth; _____

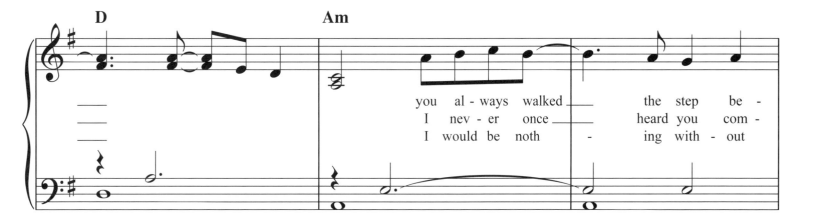

you al - ways walked _____ the step be -
I nev - er once _____ heard you com -
I would be noth - ing with - out

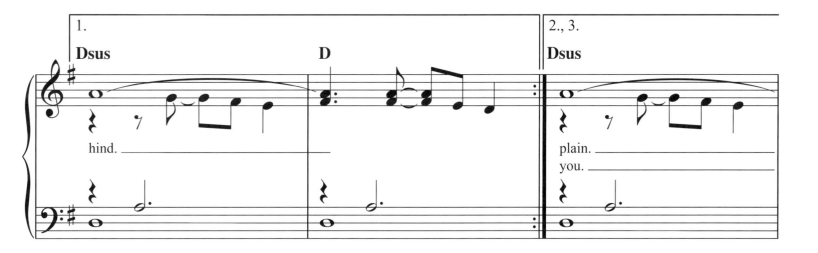

1.
hind. _____

D

2., 3.
plain. _____
you. _____

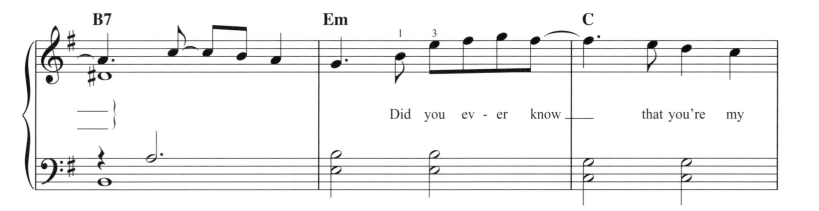

Did you ev - er know _____ that you're my

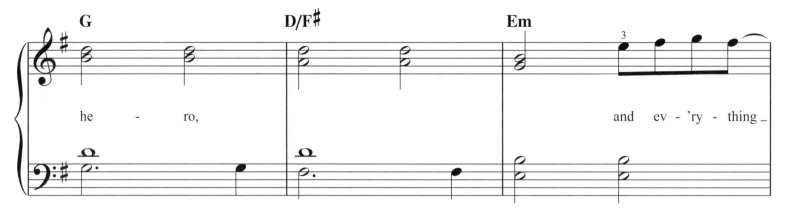

he - ro, and ev - 'ry - thing

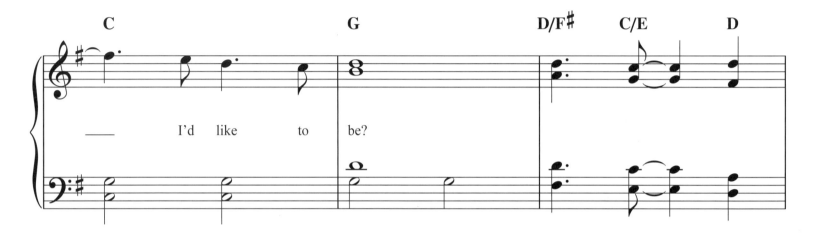

I'd like to be?

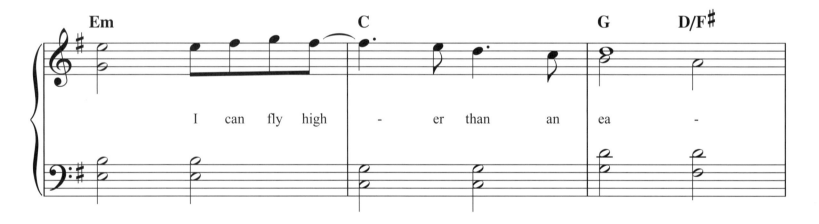

I can fly high - er than an ea -

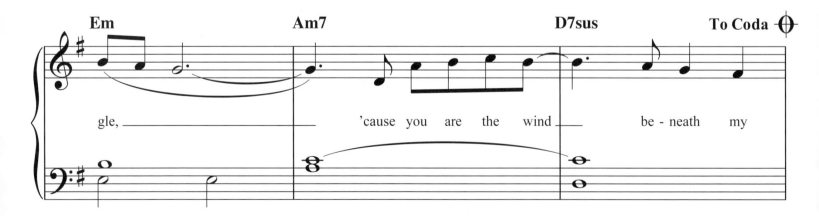

gle, 'cause you are the wind be - neath my

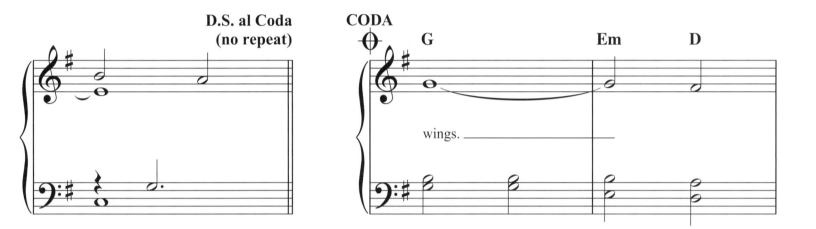

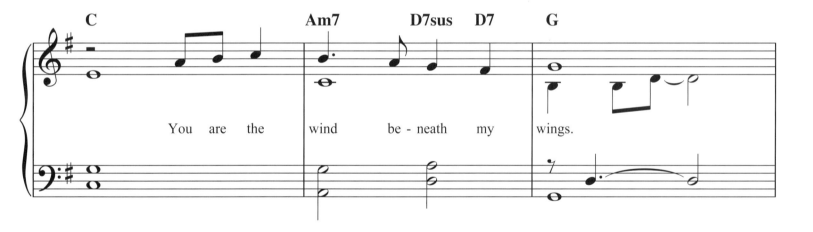

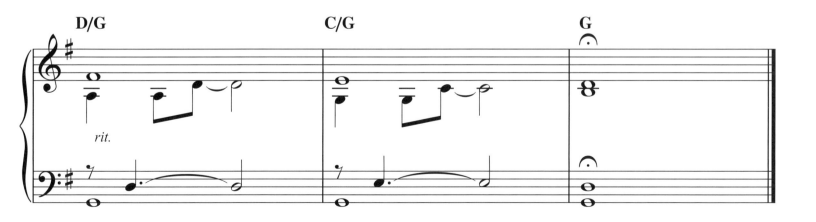

YESTERDAY

Words and Music by JOHN LENNON
and PAUL McCARTNEY

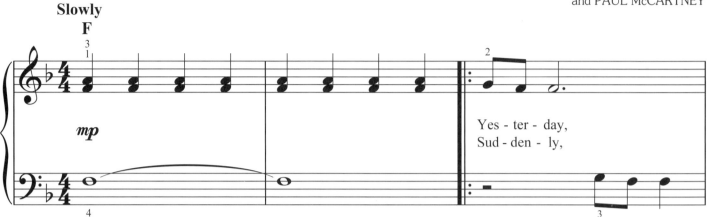

Yes - ter - day,
Sud - den - ly,

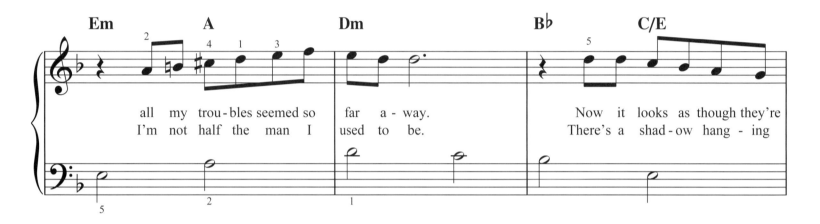

all my trou - bles seemed so far a - way.
I'm not half the man I used to be.

Now it looks as though they're
There's a shad - ow hang - ing

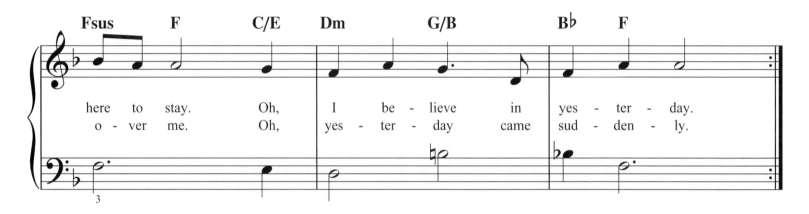

here to stay. Oh, I be - lieve in yes - ter - day.
o - ver me. Oh, yes - ter - day came sud - den - ly.

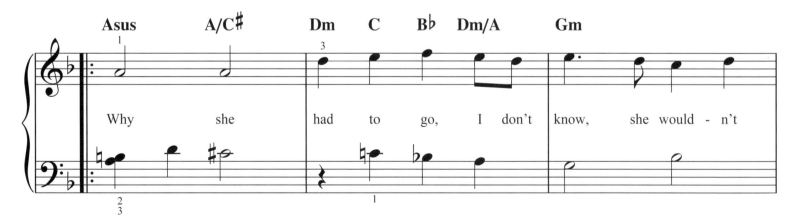

Why she had to go, I don't know, she would - n't

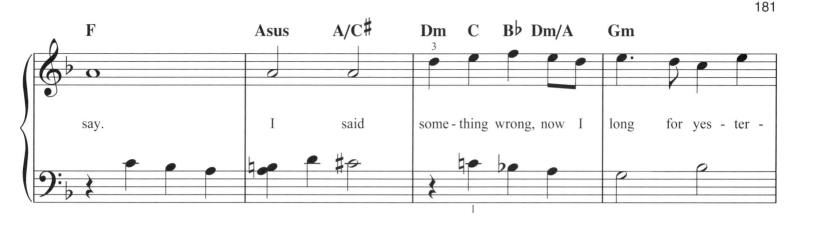

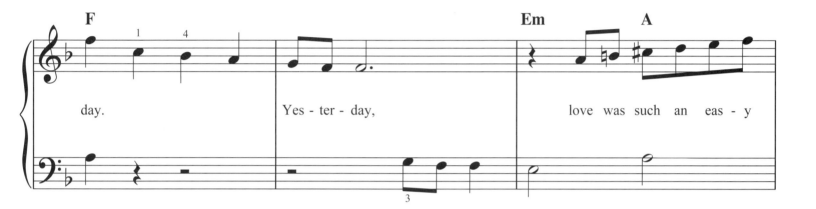

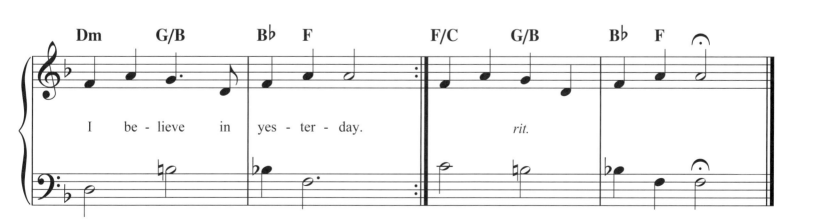

YOU SAY

Words and Music by LAUREN DAIGLE,
JASON INGRAM and PAUL MABURY

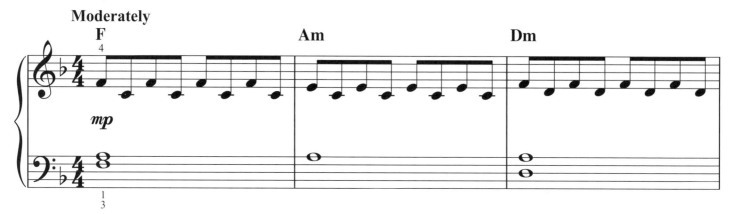

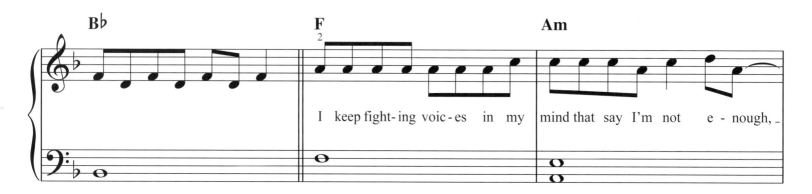

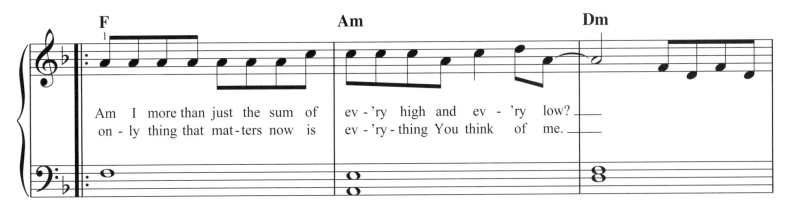

Am I more than just the sum of ev-'ry high and ev-'ry low?
on-ly thing that mat-ters now is ev-'ry-thing You think of me.

Re-mind me once a-gain just who I am, be-cause I need to know.
In You I find my worth, in You I find my i-den-ti-ty.

Ooh, oh. You say I am loved when I can't feel a

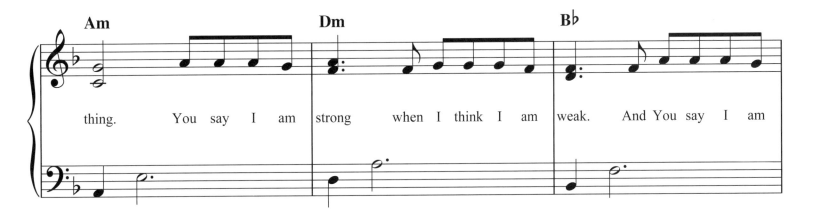

thing. You say I am strong when I think I am weak. And You say I am

held when I am fall-ing short. And when I don't be-long, oh, You say I am

To Coda

Yours, and I be-lieve, oh, I be-lieve what You say of me. I be-

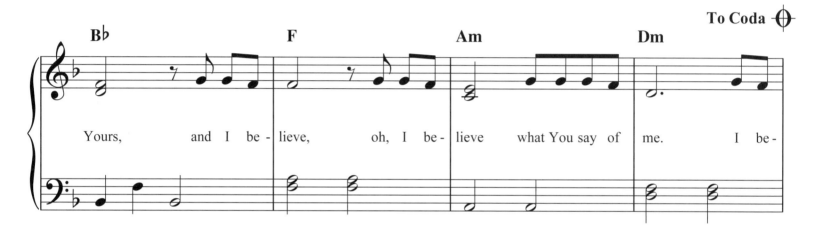

1. lieve. The lieve.

2.

Tak-ing all I have, and now I'm

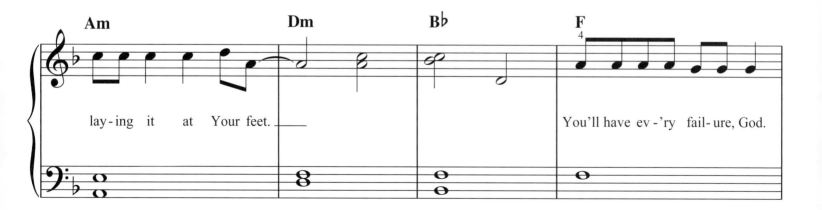

lay-ing it at Your feet.

You'll have ev-'ry fail-ure, God.

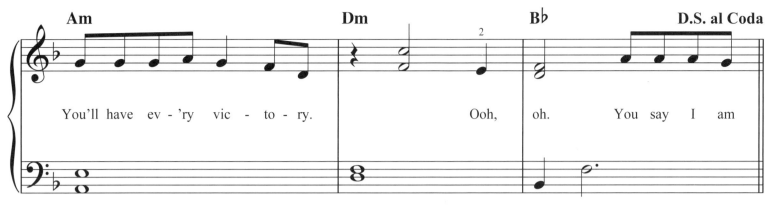

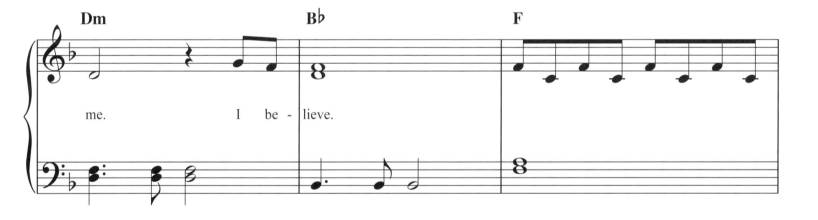

YOU'VE GOT A FRIEND

Words and Music by
CAROLE KING

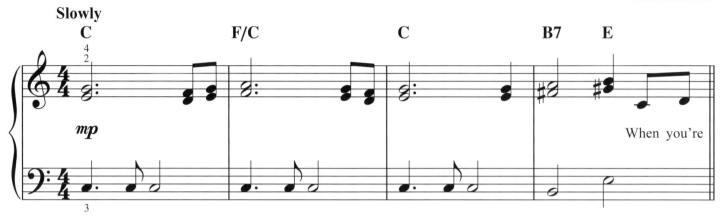

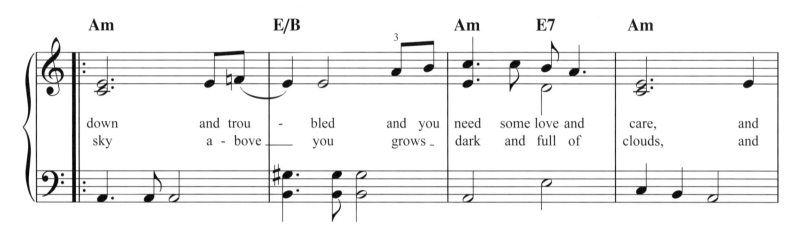

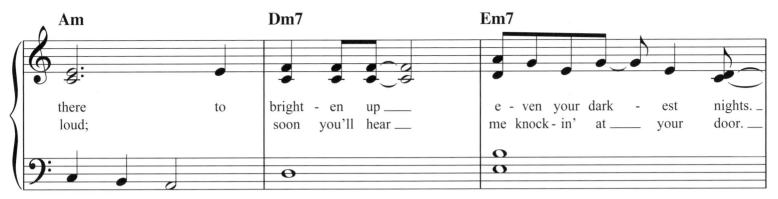

there   to   bright - en   up ____   e - ven your dark - est   nights. ____
loud;   soon you'll hear ____   me knock - in'   at ____   your   door. ____

You just   call   out my   name ____   and you

know   wher-ev - er   I   am   I'll come run - nin'   to   see you a - gain. ____

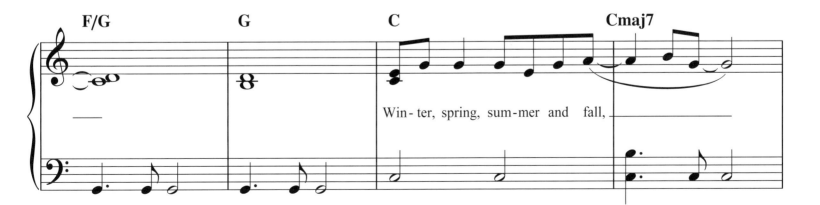

____   Win - ter, spring, sum-mer and   fall, ____

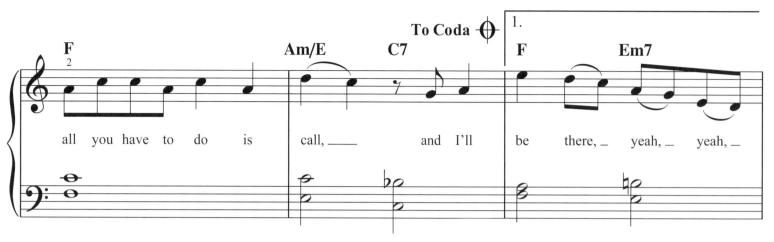

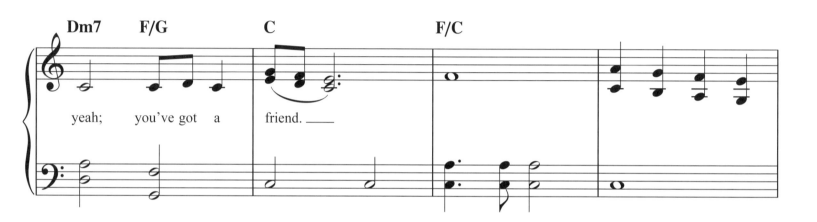

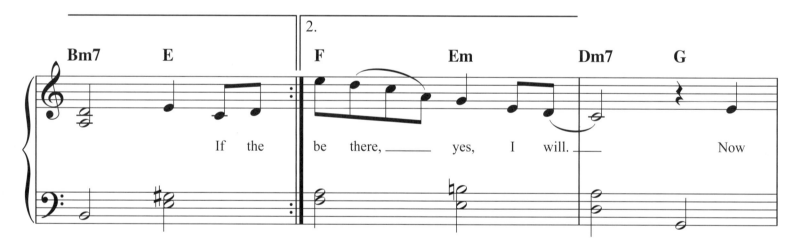

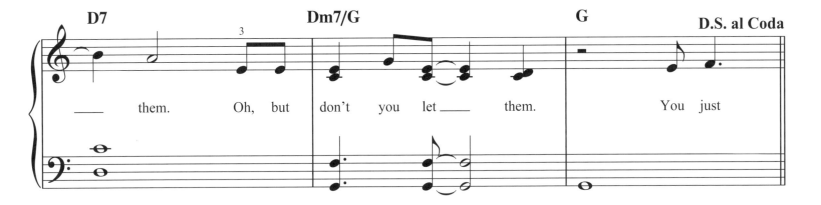

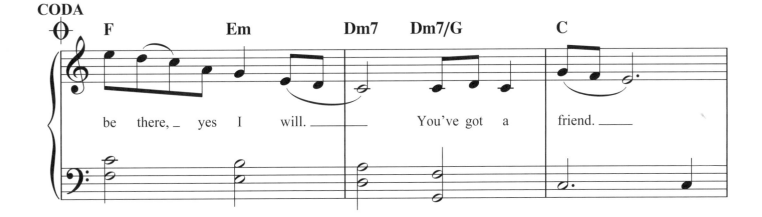

WITH YOU
from PIPPIN

Words and Music by
STEPHEN SCHWARTZ

Moderately slow

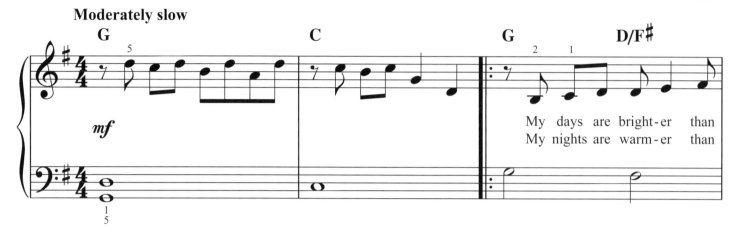

My days are bright-er than
My nights are warm-er than

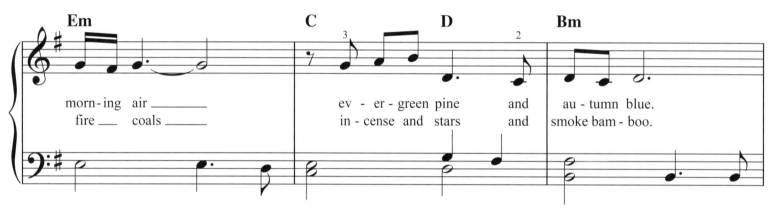

morn-ing air _____
fire ___ coals _____

ev - er - green pine and
in - cense and stars and

au - tumn blue.
smoke bam - boo.

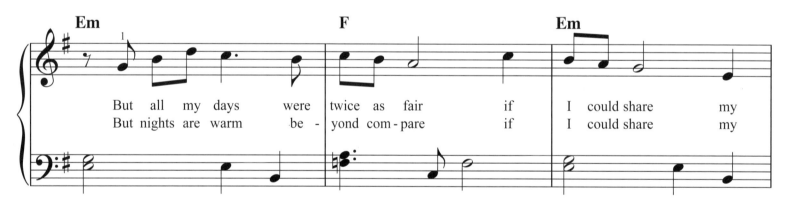

But all my days were
But nights are warm be -

twice as fair if
yond com - pare if

I could share my
I could share my

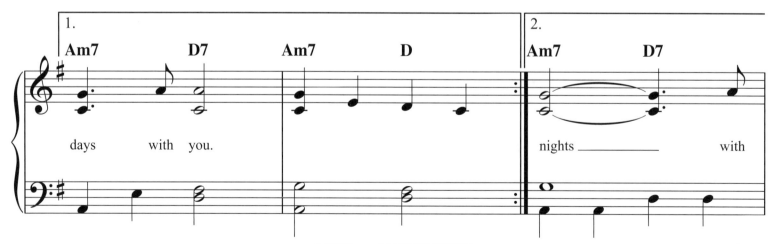

days with you.

nights _____ with

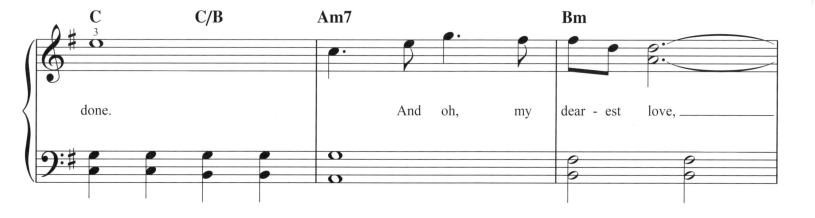

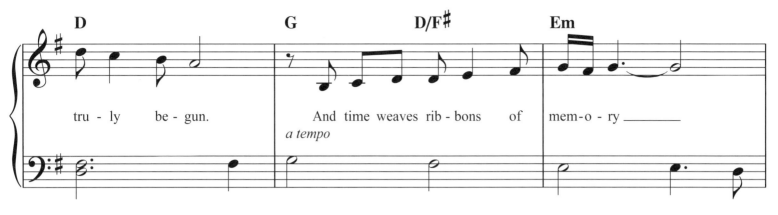

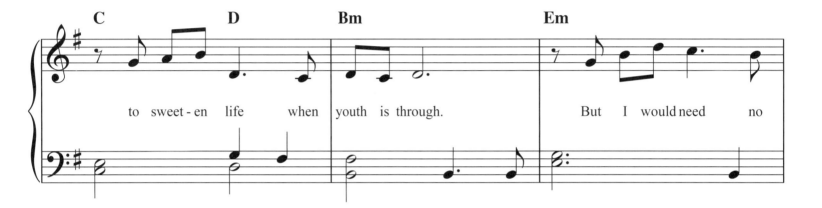

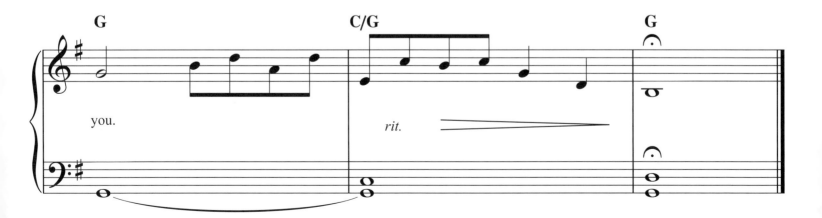